WORLD BANK WORKING PAPER NO. 118

Poverty and Regional Development in Eastern Europe and Central Asia

William Dillinger

THE WORLD BANK
Washington, D.C.

World Bank Working Papers are published to communicate the results of the Bank's work to the development community with the least possible delay. The manuscript of this paper therefore has not been prepared in accordance with the procedures appropriate to formally-edited texts. Some sources cited in this paper may be informal documents that are not readily available.

ISBN-10: 0-8213-7161-4   ISBN-13: 978-0-8213-7161-9
eISBN: 978-0-8213-7162-6
ISSN: 1726-5878   DOI: 10.1596/978-0-8213-7161-9

William Dillinger is Lead Public Sector Manager in the Poverty Reduction and Economic Management sector unit of the Europe & Central Asia regional department of the World Bank.

Library of Congress Cataloging-in-Publication Data has been requested.

Contents

Acknowledgments... v

Acronyms and Abbreviations vii

Executive Summary... ix

Introduction 1

1. What are the Objectives of Regional Development? 3

2. Regional Disparities in ECA Countries 7

3. The Market Approach 17

4. The Case for Intervention 21
   Labor Market Failures... 21
   Capital Market Failures... 24
   Coordination Failures... 26

5. Policy Instruments 29
   Macro Level Infrastructure... 29
   Education and Training.. 33
   Improving the Business Climate 34
   Firm-Specific Subsidies.. 35

6. Custom-Tailored Approaches 39
   Can Governments Pick Winners?.. 40

7. Planning and Allocating Funds for Regional Development 45
   Lessons from EU Structural Funds 46
   Improving Individual Project Evaluation 52

8. Conclusions.. 55

Bibliography 59

LIST OF TABLES

1. Correlation Between GRP per Capita and Poverty Indicators................. 9

2. Variations in Regional Poverty Indicators 11

3. Correlation Between Poverty Rate and Selected
   Regional Characteristics 14

4. Statistical Relationship Between Educational Attainment
    and Deep Poverty Rates...33

5. Average Population of Local Governments in Selected ECA Countries........46

LIST OF CHARTS

1. Economic Disparities in Selected European and Central Asian Countries........8

2A. Correlation Between GRP per Capita and Household Consumption:
    Poland...10

2B. Correlation Between GRP per Capita and Regional Poverty Levels: Poland.....10

3. Trends in Regional Economic Disparities, Large Western
    European Countries..19

4. Internal Migration Rates in Selected Countries.........................23

5. Ratio of Domestic Bank Credit to GDP.................................25

LIST OF BOXES

1. Objectives of European Regional Policy..................................5

2. Why GRP Per Capita is Not an Accurate Indicator of Poverty................11

3. Measuring Poverty..12

4. Clusters...27

5. Implicit Regional Policies...30

6. Transportation Investments are a Two-Edged Sword.......................32

7. Moldova Investment Climate Assessment................................43

8. Regional Development Agencies in Turkey..............................51

9. Project Evaluation in Chile...53

Acknowledgments

This report is ba sed on an extensive literature survey supplemented by field visits to Ireland, Spain, Turkey, and Poland. The report was prepared by William Dillinger, Task Manager. Assistance with the analysis of regional poverty data was provided by Xubei Luo, Young Professional. Formatting and editing of the report was provided by Virginia Sapinoso Yates.

Comments on earlier drafts were provided by Cheryl Gray, Sector Director, ECSPE; Pradeep Mitra, Chief Economist, ECAVP; Marsha Olive, Lead Knowledge and Learning Officer, ECAVP; Vivian Hon, Senior Economist, PRMED; Lee Travers, Sector Manager, ECSSD; Gwen Swinburn, Consultant, TUDOR; Gary Fine, Sr. Private Sector Development Specialist, ECSPS; Keith McLean, Sr. Social Development Economist, ECSSD; Yan Zhang, Urban Economist, ECSSD; Mark Sundberg, Lead Economist, DECVP; and Lili Liu, Lead Economist, PRMED; and by two external reviewers, H. W. Armstrong, Department of Geography, University of Sheffield; and Philippe Martin, Universite de Paris, France.

Additional comments on this draft were provided by Marianne Fay, Lead Economist, ECAVP; Lili Liu; Gary Fine; Marsha Olive; Carlos Felipe Jaramillo, Sector Manager, ECSPE; Lee Travers; Thomas Laursen, Lead Economist, ECSPE; Maria Donoso Clarke, Lead Social Development Specialist, ECSSD; Paula Lytle, Sr. Social Development Specialist, ECSSD; Martin Lenihan, Young Professional; and Fernando Rojas, Lead Public Sector Management Specialist, LCSPS.

The study was sponsored by the Chief Economist's Office in the Europe and Central Asia Region of the World Bank and was originally published as part of the Chief Economist's Regional Working Paper Series.

Acronyms and Abbreviations

BEEPS	Business Environment and Enterprise Performance Survey
CEE	Central and Eastern European countries
CIS	Commonwealth of Independent States
CORPO	Chilean Corporation for Development
EBRD	European Bank for Reconstruction and Development
ECAPOV	ECA Poverty Database
EU	European Union
EU10	Estonia, Latvia, Lithuania, Poland, Czech Republic, Slovakia, Hungary, Slovenia, Malta, Cyprus
FDI	Foreign Direct Investment
GRP	Gross Regional Product
IFI	International Financial Institution
IROP	Integrated Regional Operational Program
LED	Local Economic Development
NDP	National Development Plan
NUTS	European Unified System of Territorial Nomenclature
OECD	Organization for Economic Cooperation and Development
OP	Operational Program
PPP	Purchasing Power Parity
SEE	Southeastern European Countries
SPO	State Planning Organization (Turkey)

Executive Summary

Regional economic development[1] is a concern of policymakers in many ECA countries. They have a wide range of motivations. In some cases, regional development is seen as a means of reducing poverty, either in remote rural regions or in urban areas adversely affected by industrial restructuring. Efforts to disperse economic growth are also prompted by a desire to slow migration into polluted, overcrowded cities or to avoid the social costs associated with out-migration. Territorial integrity is another factor, particularly in countries with large, sparsely-populated regions (which might catch the eye of neighboring countries) or areas populated by ethnic minorities (who might be tempted to secede). Regional development is also seen as a means of stimulating economic growth—in both rich and poor regions—by taking advantage of local entities' comparative advantage in identifying constraints on growth that affect particular locations and in coordinating local responses.

This paper is focused only on the first of these objectives: the alleviation of regional concentrations of poverty. There are several reasons. First, judging from the public documents of multilaterals and governments, poverty reduction is often the primary objective of regional development efforts in the ECA region. It is also the primary objective of the World Bank, the sponsor of this paper. Second, the environmental and social objectives of regional development are difficult to analyze through an economic lens. While some may argue that cities are too big, others argue that large cities are crucial to economic growth and merely need to be better managed. By the same token, the social costs of out-migration are difficult to weigh against the economic benefits of labor mobility. The analysis of the tradeoffs between the environmental and social objectives of regional development on one hand, and economic objectives of regional development on the other, is better done on a case-by-case basis than in a regional survey paper.

Is Regional Growth an Effective Anti-poverty Strategy?

There are several well-known problems with defining regional economic growth as an anti-poverty instrument. First, it may miss the target. Although geographical concentrations of poverty do exist throughout ECA, poor people also live in regions that are—on average—rich.

Second, it may misdiagnose the sources of the problem. The available data suggest that poverty is, at best, only partly related to *where* people are. It is also strongly related to *who* people are. In the ECA region, poverty is closely associated with low levels of education and age profiles that render people too young or too old to participate in the labor force. Under these circumstances, efforts to bring better employment opportunities to poor regions may have little immediate benefit for residents who are not of working age or are unskilled. Efforts to reduce poverty should instead focus on providing income support to households with large numbers of unemployable dependents and on

---

1. "Regional development" is defined here as any effort by the public sector to stimulate economic development in specific geographical area of the national territory.

improving educational opportunities for young people and training opportunities for current members of the labor force.

Third, a narrow reliance on regional economic development to address regional concentrations of poverty ignores the potential role of migration. In regions with few economic prospects, the out-migration of labor—rather than the in-migration of capital—is likely to be a more effective means of addressing the poverty of individuals. Levels of interregional migration in the ECA countries are low by international standards. But governments can reduce barriers to migration in several ways. Labor market liberalization can increase employment opportunities in potential destination regions. Reforms in social benefits can reduce disincentives to move. Housing market reforms can reduce the cost of housing in destination regions. Rural land adjudication can provide potential migrants with a stake to finance the costs of relocation. And investments in human capital—in education and skills training— can increase the likelihood that people in poor regions will have access to better-paying jobs once they migrate.

There are nevertheless valid arguments for extending special treatment to regions with high concentrations of poverty. Out-migration alone is unlikely to eliminate pockets of poverty within a relevant time frame. It is also conceivable that development opportunities exist in poor regions that markets may have overlooked. The underdeveloped domestic capital markets of the ECA countries are unlikely to seek out high risk investments on their own initiative. And neither domestic nor foreign investors can be expected to address regional deficiencies in infrastructure and human capital. As a result, efforts to address poverty through regional economic development may, under some circumstances, contribute to growth in the economy as a whole.

Forms of Intervention

Efforts at intervention have to be carefully assessed in terms of their effectiveness. The literature on economic geography argues fairly persuasively that, in market economies, economic activity locates where it does for very good reasons. Scholars argue over the nature of initial comparative advantages and the relative importance of plant-level, industry-level, and city-level agglomeration economies. But few dispute the view that economic imperatives cause economic activity to concentrate in some regions and not in others. It follows that government efforts to alter the location of economic activity are likely to be ineffective or extremely expensive—both in terms of the government's budget and in terms of the efficiency of the economy as a whole.

The literature also suggests that some of the traditional instruments used to stimulate regional economic growth are not particularly effective. Highway investments, in particular, can be a two-edged sword, opening new markets to a region's exports but exposing its existing industries to competition from more efficient producers from outside the region. Investments in power and telecommunications have an impact only if they address binding constraints. Education helps but only if it imparts skills relevant to the marketplace. Firm-specific investment incentives also have a mixed track record. The evidence suggests that such incentives can affect investors' location decisions, if the incentives are large enough. But they do not guarantee that the resulting investments will have broader multiplier effects on the regional economy. Or that the investors will remain once the incentives expire.

Comprehensive, custom-tailored approaches appear to be a promising alternative. In principle, these are based on detailed diagnoses of the specific impediments to growth in a particular region. They define key growth sectors and actions to be taken by the full range of relevant actors in both public and private sectors to overcome these constraints. But it is not clear that comprehensive strategies are actually feasible. Efforts by governments to pick "growth sectors" have a decidedly mixed track record. Consensus among the relevant stakeholders may be difficult to reach. It is also not clear that countries are organized to implement regional strategies. Many of the determinants of regional growth lie outside the reach of local institutions. Public expenditures in ECA countries are dominated by national sectoral ministries which tend to function in sectoral stovepipes. While municipal governments would seem to be well-positioned to take a cross-sectoral view of development, they tend to have little influence over the major determinants of growth and are too small, in geographical terms, to take a regional perspective. Efforts to create new entities at the regional level run the risk of creating political orphans—ignored by both national sectoral ministries and the local governments whose efforts they are supposed to coordinate.

Conclusion

Governments should therefore be modest in using regional development as a tool of poverty alleviation Focusing on geographically-defined units of analysis can be a useful device for identifying constraints on growth that affect particular locations. Under some circumstances, it can be a useful means of targeting poverty whose particular cause is location specific. But policies aimed at stimulating growth in poor regions have to be complemented by more direct anti-poverty measures, including the improved targeting of transfers to low income households and investments in education and skills. Barriers to the out-migration of labor must be reduced. And barriers to the in-migration of capital—including national level reforms in the financial sector, in business regulation, and in the organizations responsible for the timely provision of infrastructure and social services—must also be considered.

This report is the first of a series of papers on regional issues in the ECA region. Subsequent papers will delve further into local economic development efforts and the social, cultural, and environmental aspects of regional development.

Introduction

Regional economic development[2] is a concern of policymakers in many of the ECA countries. In some cases these concerns focus areas of long-standing rural poverty. In others, they focus on cities adversely affected by industrial restructuring. Governments have often responded to these concerns by attempting to stimulate economic growth in these locations. Focusing on geographically-defined units of analysis can be a useful device for identifying constraints on growth that affect particular locations. Under some circumstances, it can be a useful means of targeting poverty whose particular cause is location specific. It can therefore be useful to learn from successful examples of regional development. Many such efforts involve costly programs of infrastructure investment and subsidies to private firms. Some are ineffective. Some are actively harmful to the national economy as a whole. Governments need to understand the impact of such programs in order to find less costly ways of achieving their objectives.

---

2. "Regional development" is defined here as any effort by the public sector to stimulate economic development in specific geographical area of the national territory.

CHAPTER 1

What are the Objectives of Regional Development?

Governments pursue a variety of objectives under the rubric of regional development. Judging from the public documents of multilaterals and governments in the ECA region, one of the primary objectives of regional development in the ECA region is poverty reduction. In the European Union (EU), this is couched in terms of "convergence." Elsewhere it is expressed as the problem of lagging regions or one-industry towns. The aim is to address poverty *in situ* by reviving the economies of specific geographical areas.

There are several well-known problems with defining regional economic growth as a policy objective. As a strategy for poverty reduction, it may miss the target. Although geographical concentrations of poverty do exist throughout ECA, poor people also live in regions that are—on average—rich. Poland's poorest region, for example, accounts for only three percent of Poland's poor—less than a third of the number of poor residing in its richest region.[3] Only 17 percent of Turkey's poor live in its poorest region (Eastern Anatolia); a figure not much greater than the number of poor residing in the richest region, Marmara. Focusing poverty reduction efforts on the poorest region would therefore appear to bypass a large proportion of the target.

Efforts directed at regional concentrations of poverty may also misdiagnose the sources of the problem. The available data suggest that poverty is, at best, only partly related to where people are. It is also strongly related to *who* people are. While it can be argued that regional concentrations of poverty reflect the particular disadvantages of certain regions—remoteness, absence of infrastructure, limited local consumer demand—it can also be argued that regional poverty is a reflection of the characteristics of the people who live there: low levels of education or age profiles that render them too young or too old to participate in the labor force.

---

3. Based on the most comprehensive measure of poverty (WB-2), see World Bank 2004a.

Under the latter circumstances, efforts to bring higher-wage employment to poor regions may have little benefit for the resident population. If people characteristics, rather than place characteristics, are the overriding explanation for regional concentrations of poverty, it suggests that efforts to reduce poverty should focus on improving the educational level of the labor force and on providing income support to households with large numbers of unemployable dependents, rather than on attracting new sources of high wage employment for which the resident population may not be qualified.

There is a third drawback to relying on regional economic development to address regional concentrations of poverty: it ignores the potential role of migration. In regions with few economic prospects, the out-migration of labor—rather than the in-migration of capital—is likely to be a more effective means of reducing the poverty of individuals. A regional policy that includes the depopulation of some lagging regions is therefore entirely consistent with the objective of poverty reduction.

Other Objectives of Regional Development

Poverty reduction is not the sole objective of regional development. Regional development is also pursued as a means of promoting national or local economic growth. Growth-oriented regional development comes in several varieties. One is aimed at unlocking the potential of resource-rich regions. This form of regional development is exemplified by large scale public works projects—the trans-Amazon Highway in Brazil, the Tennessee Valley Authority in the United States, the Southeastern Anatolia Irrigation Project (GAP) in southeastern Turkey. The French effort to create a Gallic Silicon Valley at Sophia Antipolis had a similar motivation. The growth objective has its smaller scale equivalent in local government efforts to promote the growth of local economies in order to provide job opportunities for their citizens and to strengthen local tax bases. As characterized by the Bank's local economic development (LED) website, "the purpose of local economic development is to build up the economic capacity of a local area to improve its economic future and the quality of life for all. It is a process by which public, business, and non-governmental sector partners work collectively to create better conditions for economic growth and employment generation."[4] These motivations are relevant in all regions, rich and poor alike.

There are also socio-political motivations. Efforts to promote growth in lagging regions are often prompted by a fear that a failure to do so will prompt a mass migration of the destitute into overcrowded cities. Territorial integrity is another factor, particularly in countries with large underpopulated regions (which might catch the eye of neighboring countries) or areas populated by ethnic minorities (who are threatening to secede). Critics of the EU's regional development efforts have argued that its objective has less to do with poverty reduction and more to do with the need to induce Spain, Portugal, and Greece (and now the more recent accession members) to make the economic adjustments required for their entry into the EU—which in turn had as its goal the expansion of the EU market (for the benefit of all members) and the prevention of another European conflict. Most recently, interest in

---

4. http://web.worldbank.org/WBSITE/EXTERNAL/TOPICS/EXTURBANDEVELOPMENT/EXTLED.

Box 1. Objectives of European Regional Policy

The regional policies of the European Union focus on growth as well as poverty reduction and are attuned to a variety of different circumstances. As stated in documents of the Directorate of Regional Policy, the Union seeks to use the (regional) policy to help lagging regions to catch up, restructure declining industrial regions, diversify the economies of rural areas with declining agriculture and revitalize declining neighborhoods in the cities. In line with the renewed Lisbon strategy, programs co-financed through (regional funds) target resources on the following three priorities: improving the attractiveness of member states, regions and cities by improving accessibility, ensuring adequate quality and level of services, and preserving their environmental potential; encouraging innovation, entrepreneurship and the growth of the knowledge economy by research and innovation capacities, including new information and communication technologies; and creating more and better jobs by attracting more people into employment entrepreneurial activity, improving adaptability of workers and enterprises, and increasing investment in human capital.

Source: European Commission: Regional Policy Directorate website: http://ec.europa.eu/ regional_policy/intro/working1_en.htm and "Community Strategic Guidelines on Cohesion 2007–2013."

---

regional development has been sparked by financial considerations. Recent and prospective EU countries have taken up regional development in order to qualify for EU Structural Funds.

Not all these objectives are mutually compatible. For example, a recent high-level review of EU policies report (Sapir 2003), argues that efforts to stimulate the growth of lagging regions are likely to undermine national economic growth. "Policies oriented toward maintaining what is socially regarded as an adequate degree of cohesion may reduce the efficiency and growth benefits arising from market liberalization and integration. Policies carried out at the EU level have interfered with the specialization of regions in the aftermath of economic integration, and quite deliberately so, since such policies were aimed at preventing agglomeration in the first place."

This paper will focus exclusively on only one of the motivations for regional development: alleviating regional concentrations of poverty. To this end, it will address three questions: (1) Is poverty geographically concentrated in the ECA region? (2) To the extent that it is, should governments focus on addressing poverty in situ, or on encouraging outmigration? (3) To the extent that governments should focus on addressing poverty in situ, what are the most effective, and least costly, means of doing so?

CHAPTER 2

Regional Disparities in ECA Countries

Whether there are regional pockets of poverty in ECA depends on how pockets are defined and how poverty is defined. Chart 1, below, suggests that regional economic disparities in the larger countries of Eastern Europe are roughly on a par with those of their counterparts in Western Europe, while disparities in Turkey, Russia, and Kazakhstan are considerably wider. These results vary, depending on the definition of geographical units and the indicator that is used to measure poverty.

Defining Regions

Regional descriptors are sensitive to geographic scale. In general, variations appear wider when geographical units are defined on a smaller scale. Measured at the NUTS2 level France's richest region is twice as wealthy (in GRP per capita terms) as its poorest.[5] Measured at the NUTS1 level the discrepancy falls to 1.2:1. In Bulgaria, the NUTS3 definition produces a discrepancy of 3:1. Under the NUTS2 definition, the discrepancy falls to 1.8:1. In Russia, the richest of the seven administrative regions has a GRP per capita 2.3 times that of the poorest. The discrepancy is ten times as large between the richest and the poorest of the 88 individual units of federation.

For purposes of this analysis, the ideal definition of a region would be a commuter-shed. Advocates of regional economic equality argue that people should not have to migrate to find high-wage employment—jobs should come to people rather than people coming to jobs. A region should therefore be defined as the geographical area that permits everyone residing

---

5. NUTS is the acronym for the European standard territorial classification system.

in the region to reach all employment opportunities in the region without changing residences. (For the UK, it has been suggested that a 45-minute driving time would be an appropriate definition; see Rice, Venables, and Pattachine 2006). No such territorial organization exists in the databases used for this study.[6] For purposes of this analysis, the available regional data is organized using the European standard territorial classification system, NUTS, for those countries where this classification is available. The NUTS system defines regions on the basis of population. NUTS1 regions range from

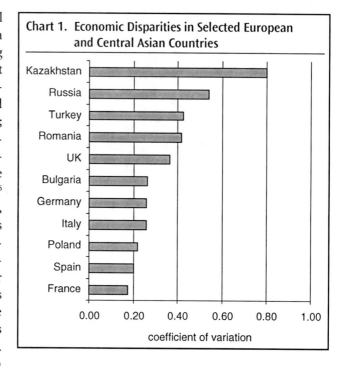

Chart 1. Economic Disparities in Selected European and Central Asian Countries

3 million to 7 million; NUTS2 regions from 800,000 to 3 million, and NUTS3 regions from 150,000 to 800,000. (Due to data constraints, most of the analysis in this study is conducted at the NUTS2 level, although these can be large—certainly far beyond 45 minutes driving time—in sparsely populated areas.) The Russia data is organized on the basis of the country's seven administrative regions, with further analysis on the basis of individual units of federation (i.e., the 88 autonomous republics, oblasts, counties, and other jurisdictions comprising the federation). To eliminate outliers, nine entities with populations under 75,000 and/or very high resource-based per capita gross regional products (GRPs) are excluded. For Kazakhstan, regions are defined on the basis of existing political subdivisions (14 oblasts plus the cities of Astana and Almaty). In Tajikistan, regions are defined on the basis of political subdivisions: three oblasts, the capital of Dushanbe, and the rayons of republic subordination (as a group) surrounding the capital.

Defining Poverty

The scale of regional disparities also depends on how poverty is defined. The most widely used indicator of regional poverty is an economic one: gross regional product per capita. On

---

6. This analysis is based on six of the seven largest countries (in territorial terms) in the ECA region for which regional economic and poverty data are both available: Bulgaria, Kazakhstan, Poland, Romania, Russia, and Turkey. Regionalized data on GRP and poverty is also available for territorially smaller countries, including Hungary, Latvia, and Lithuania, but was not analyzed. Limited information is also provided on Tajikistan, where regionalized poverty data is available but regionalized data on GRP is not. More detailed data is provided on Poland, taking advantage of recent reports on regional development (World Bank 2004a, 2004c).

this basis, there are indeed pockets of poverty—or at least wide economic disparities—within the countries of the ECA region. As shown in Chart 1, the coefficient of variation in regional per capita income ranges from a low of .22 in Poland to a high of .80 in Kazakhstan. In general, regional economic variations are higher in ECA countries than in Western Europe. Although the coefficients of variation in gross regional product per capita in Poland and Bulgaria are roughly on a par with those of western European countries, they are considerably larger in Romania and Turkey, and are particularly large in Russia and Kazakhstan—even allowing for the impact of oil and gas extraction on the GRPs of certain jurisdictions in the Urals and Siberia.

In geographic terms, high levels of GRP per capita are generally associated with large cities and with capital cities in particular. Mazowieckie, the region containing Warsaw, is the richest region in Poland. Bulgaria's southwest region (containing Sofia) is its richest. Bucharest is the richest region in Romania; Marmara (containing Istanbul) is Turkey's richest. In Russia, greater Moscow is the richest region, once sparsely populated oil and gold extracting regions are excluded. (St. Petersburg is a somewhat distant second.) In Kazakhstan, the commercial capital (Almaty) and the political capital (Astana) are the richest jurisdictions, once the oil-rich oblasts of Atyrau and Mangystau are excluded.

Economic backwardness, on the other hand, has no simple geographical correlates—other than an absence of capital cities. In Eastern Europe and Turkey, it tends to be associated with proximity to a poorer (eastern) neighbor. Poland's four poorest regions lie on its eastern and northern borders with Belarus, Ukraine and Russia (Kaliningrad). Romania's poorest region lies on its eastern border with Moldova. Turkey's poorest regions lie on its eastern borders with Syria, Iran, and Armenia. In Russia, economic backwardness is clearly associated with the south. Six of Russia's eight poorest regions are in the Caucasus. Kazakhstan's poorest region, similarly, lies on its border with Kyrgyzstan.

But GRP per capita is an imperfect indicator of the welfare of individuals. Table 1 shows the correlation of GRP per capita and three standard indicators of household welfare—

Table 1. Correlation Between GRP per Capita and Poverty Indicators			
Country	Household Consumption	Moderate Poverty	Deep Poverty
Poland	+.78	−.37	−.30
Bulgaria	+.79	−.77	−.69
Romania	+.96	−.88	−.92
Turkey	+.93	−.81	−.91
Russia	+.59	−.40	−.46
Kazakhstan	+.33	−.47	−.33

*Household expenditure is adjusted for regional variations in cost of living. Poland data is based on Living Standards report and includes housing and consumer durables.

household consumption, moderate poverty, and deep poverty. As shown, the strength of the correlation varies considerably among countries. In Bulgaria, Romania, and Turkey, regional variations in GRP per capita are highly correlated with regional variations in household consumption and poverty. The correlation coefficients for all three indicators range from .69 to

.96. The relationship is considerably weaker in Poland. Although variations in GRP per capita are correlated with variations in household consumption (Chart 2A), the relationship between GRP and poverty levels is relatively weak (Chart 2B). The relationship is also weak in Russia and Kazakhstan.

As described in Box 2, there are several explanations for such discrepancies. The transfer of profits derived from resource extraction to owners outside the region may explain the weak correlation between GRP and household consumption in Russian and Kazakhstan. Regional variations in prices also appear to be an important factor in Russia. (The correlation between GRP per capita and household consumption rises to .79 if household consumption is not corrected for regional variations in prices.)

If the objective of regional development is to reduce regional disparities in living standards, then measures-based household consumption are a more appropriate indicator. These measures yield a considerably different depiction of the landscape. As shown in Table 2, regional variations in per capita household consumption are considerably smaller than those in GRP per

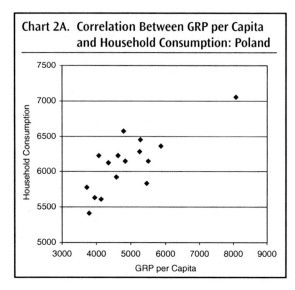

Chart 2A. Correlation Between GRP per Capita and Household Consumption: Poland

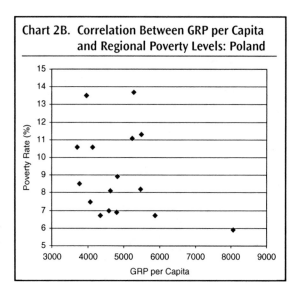

Chart 2B. Correlation Between GRP per Capita and Regional Poverty Levels: Poland

capita. Coefficients of variation in per capita household consumption range from .07 in Poland to .25 in Turkey. In the Eastern European countries analyzed for this report there is virtually no variation in average per capita household consumption—the coefficients of variation range from .07 to .10. Even in Russia, Turkey, and the Central Asian countries, regional disparities in household consumption are fairly modest. The coefficient of variation in household consumption does not exceed .25 for this group of countries.

There is also relatively little variation in moderate poverty. Coefficients of variation range from a low of .04 in Tajikistan (everyone is poor) to a high of .26 in Kazakhstan. Levels of deep poverty however, show substantial variations among regions, with coefficients of variation ranging from .22 in Tajikistan to .58 in Kazakhstan. In Poland, 14 percent of the population of the eastern region Warminsko-Mazurskie live in deep poverty,

Box 2. Why GRP Per Capita is Not an Accurate Indicator of Poverty

GRP per capita is not an accurate indicator of poverty. There are several reasons. By definition, GRP, as calculated on an output basis, should be equal to GRP calculated on income basis. This might suggest that the two should be correlated—that income generated by regional production units would be reflected in the income of households within the region. But this relationship applies only to the proportion of GRP that constitutes returns to labor—compensation to employees and the incomes of self-employed persons. GRP also includes the gross operating surpluses of firms. Although this may be paid out in stock dividends or interest payments (or held as retained earnings) it does not necessarily accrue to households in the region. In fact, it may not accrue to households located in the country, if the firm is owned or financed by overseas investors. GRP also includes taxes, which in the ECA countries consume a significant share of the gross operating surpluses generated by production units. As the majority of taxes are collected and spent by central governments, they are unlikely to contribute directly to the income of households in the region.

Household income, on the other hand, includes not only returns to labor but also income from transfer payments. These include social protection payments such as pensions, social assistance, and unemployment benefits. (As noted above, the tax payments that finance these transfers are reflected in the GRP of the region in which they are generated, not in the region to which the payments were made.) They also include income from remittances. If returns to capital and taxes are disproportionately generated in a rich region and social protection payments and remittances are disproportionately received in a poorer one, this would result in significant discrepancies between regional patterns of economic development and regional patterns of household income or poverty.

Regional variations in prices may also undermine the correlation. Regional variations in the cost of living are not reflected in GRP calculations but are reflected in the data sets used to measure household expenditure and poverty rates in this report. Regional variations in unemployment rates, labor force participation rates, and dependency ratios could play a similar role. For any given level of gross regional product per capita, a high unemployment rate, a low labor force participation rate, or a high dependency ratio will increase levels of poverty.

In theory, commuting could also distort the relationship between GRP per capita and poverty. In calculating GRPs, production is recorded at the place of work. Poverty statistics, on the other hand, are based on the place of residence. Thus regions with high inflows of productive commuters might have high GRPs but relatively low levels of per capita household income. This is not likely to be a major factor in the data set used for this report, however. As noted below, the scale of regions used in this report is large and presumably encompasses both the workplace and residence of most commuters.

Table 2. Variations in Regional Poverty Indicators

| | Coefficients of Variation | | | | Percent of Population in Deep Poverty in: | |
	GDP/ Capita	HH Consumption	Moderate Poverty	Deep Poverty	Richest Region	Poorest Region
Poland	0.22	0.07	0.19	0.27	1	5
Bulgaria	0.26	0.07	0.14	0.33	2	7
Romania	0.42	0.10	0.15	0.37	4	18
Russia	0.58	0.18	0.16	0.39	0	25
Turkey	0.38	0.25	0.24	0.55	8	39
Kazakhstan	0.80	0.24	0.26	0.58	2	38
Tajikistan	NA	0.22	0.04	0.22	53	88

Box 3. Measuring Poverty

For this study, poverty is defined on the basis of the consumption, using the definitions and statistics compiled for the recent report on poverty in the ECA region (World Bank 2004a). The poverty rate—headcount poverty—is measured as a percent of the population living in households with per capita household consumption below specified thresholds. The threshold for moderate poverty is PPP$4.30. For deep poverty, it is PPP$2.15.

There are several important limitations to this data. First, in the absence of reliable data on income, it is based on consumption. Income devoted to savings or transfers to persons not living in the household are therefore excluded from the calculation. The consumption figure, in turn, reflects only a subset of consumption items. Three particular items are excluded: housing (other than utilities), consumer durables, and health care. As a result, the poverty indicator is dominated by household expenditures on food. In Bulgaria, Romania, and Russia, food (together with alcohol and tobacco) accounts for roughly 55 percent of measured household expenditures. In Turkey and Poland, it accounts for about forty percent.[7] While the exclusion of housing, consumer durables, and health care may not distort poverty rates in very poor countries, it might be expected to do so in middle income countries, where the ability to buy food is not the characteristic that distinguishes the poor from the rest of the population.

Poverty rates also appear to be sensitive to household composition. In the ECAPOV database, no allowance is made for household composition. For any given level of total household expenditure, a household with four members is twice as poor as a household with two. This may exaggerate the impact of household size on living conditions. Poverty indicators used in the recent World Bank report (2004a) on Poland, for example, reflect the rules of the Polish social assistance system. These assume that the marginal cost of maintaining a household declines with household size. This (along with differences in PPP conversion factors) may explain why the average poverty rate in Poland using the ECAPOV definition is three times the rate reported in the recent Poland report, even at similar thresholds (PPP$4.30 per capita versus PPP$ 5.50) and equivalent consumption baskets.

---

as opposed to just six percent in the region encompassing Warsaw. In the northeast region of Romania, 18 percent of the population is classified as poor, as compared to four percent in Bucharest. In Bulgaria, seven percent of the population in the south-central region (including Sofia) is classified as deeply poor, compared to just two percent of the population of the region encompassing Sofia. Dagestan, in the south of Russia has a poverty rate of 25 percent, compared with a 0 percent rate in St. Petersburg. South Kazakhstan oblast has a 39 percent poverty rate, compared with a two percent rate in Astana.

Overall, this yields two conclusions. First, for the majority of the populations of the countries under study, regional variations in living conditions are nowhere near as wide as regional variations in gross regional products per capita. Some combination of the factors described in Box 2—the "export" of profits from resource-rich regions, social assistance payments to households in poor regions, regional variations in living costs, etc.—is apparently at work. But the analysis also shows that regions do exist within each of these countries that contain unusually large concentrations of people in deep poverty. In this sense, pockets of poverty do exist.

Why are people in poor regions poor? Are regional concentrations of poverty due to place characteristics or people characteristics? It can be argued that regional concentrations

---

7. In the ECAPOV and Poland databases, the imputed value of food grown for own consumption is included in the calculation of household consumption.

of poverty, to the extent they exist, reflect an absence of economic opportunities. In this sense, poverty would be expected to be associated with high levels of unemployment or an absence of higher-wage job opportunities. Such circumstances might justify a strategy aimed at attracting better jobs to a poor region. It can also be argued that a region's poverty is a reflection of the characteristics of the people who live there—age profiles that render them too young or too old to participate in the labor force, low levels of education that prevent them from qualifying for higher wage employment. Under the latter circumstances, efforts to bring higher wage employment to poor regions may have little benefit for the resident population.[8]

A recent World Bank survey (2005b) of poverty in the ECA region identified four characteristics that account for much of the variation in poverty rates among *individuals*. The first is employment status—whether the individual in question is unemployed. This has a particularly strong explanatory power in the more industrialized countries of the region. In Poland, 37 percent of the unemployed are classified as poor,[9] compared to seven percent of the employed. In Bulgaria, 12 percent of unemployed adults are poor, compared to two percent of wage employees and the self-employed. In Russia, 16 percent of unemployed adults are classified as poor. This is more than twice the poverty rate of wage employees (7 percent) or the self-employed (7 percent). Similar patterns are reported for Romania and Kazakhstan.

Unemployment has less explanatory power in countries with larger rural populations. In Turkey, 13 percent of the unemployed are poor, a figure roughly equal to the poverty rate among wage earners (12 percent) and well below the figure for the self employed (21 percent). In Tajikistan, the level of poverty among the unemployed (79 percent) is only slightly higher than that of wage employees (72 percent) or the self-employed (68 percent). This is because in countries with weak or non-existent social safety nets, open unemployment is not an economically viable option. Instead, low-productivity employment acts as an income source of last resort.

Rural location is the second correlate of poverty identified in the World Bank poverty report. In Russia, the rural poverty rate is 14 percent, compared with five percent in Moscow, and seven percent in other urban areas. In Romania, the rural poverty rate is 20 percent, compared to four percent in Bucharest and six to seven percent in other urban areas. In Poland, the rural poverty rate (12 percent) is nearly twice the level of the urban rate (7 percent). In Turkey, the rural poverty rate (24 percent) is significant higher than in urban areas (18 percent) and three times the level in Ankara and Istanbul. The link between poverty and rural location lies in part in the sectoral composition of rural employment. Agriculture is the dominant sector of employment in rural areas and offers less lucrative employment options compared to formal sector employment in urban areas.[10]

---

8. In principle, bringing in higher wage employment could benefit local unskilled workers, either indirectly or over the long term. Purchases of intermediate inputs by the new firms—and spending by their employees—could increase demand for locally produced goods and services, including those produced by the less skilled. 'Modern' firms could also stimulate local innovation by example. But these indirect and long term benefits have to be weighed against their immediate costs—and the risk that they may never materialize.

9. Meaning that 37 percent of unemployed adults live in households in which the level of per capita household consumption falls below the poverty line.

10. But not always. In Poland, the poverty level of farm workers is 9.06 percent, not much above the 7.5 percent rate among wage earners The poverty rate for farm *owners* is 7.6 percent.

Low levels of education are strongly correlated with poverty—in some countries. In Bulgaria, adults with less than a primary education run a 14 percent chance of being poor (and account for half the total number of poor adults). Adults with a primary education run a five percent risk of poverty; those with a general secondary education, a two percent chance. Similarly, in Turkey, the poverty rate among those without a primary education is 30 percent, compared with 17 percent for those with a primary education, and seven percent for those with a secondary general education. But there are exceptions. In Russia, educational attainment (at least below the tertiary level) has no impact on poverty rates. The poverty level of adults with basic education (seven percent) is roughly the same as those with secondary general education (8 percent) and secondary vocational education (6 percent). (The number of adults with less than a primary education is negligible.)

Large household size is the fourth major correlate of poverty. This is because large households have large numbers of dependents—children too young to work or adults too old to work. Household size affects poverty rates in all the countries reviewed for this study. In Russia, the poverty rate for large households (those with three or more children) is 27 percent, compared to nine percent for households with one or two children, and four percent for households with no children. In Romania, the poverty rate of large households is 54 percent, compared with 14 percent for small households with one or two children and five percent with no children. In Turkey, the poverty rate is 50 percent for large households, 38 percent for small households, and twelve percent for households with no children.

These four factors partially explain regional variations in levels of deep poverty. Some poor regions do have relatively high levels of unemployment. Some are more rural. In some cases, their labor forces are less educated. Many have relatively large households. But the statistical relationship between these characteristics and regional poverty rates is generally weak. As shown in Table 3, high levels unemployment are associated with high levels of poverty in Poland, Russia, and Turkey. But the relationship is reversed in Bulgaria and Romania. In those countries, high levels of unemployment are associated (although weakly) with *low* levels of poverty. In Tajikistan, similarly, regions with high unemployment levels have low lev-

Table 3. Correlation Between Poverty Rate and Selected Regional Characteristics

	No. of Regions	Unemployment Rate	Percent Rural	Education*	HH Size
Poland	16	.45	−.10	−.12	.21
Bulgaria					
NUTS2	6	−.29	.92	.05	−.17
NUTS3	28	.26	.11	.01	.36
Romania	8	−.22	.89	−.91	.82
Russia	79	.65	.54	−.29	.55
Turkey	7	.43	.42	−.83	.88
Kazakhstan	16	.38	.63	−.33	na
Tajikistan	5	−.58	.65	−.06	.06

*Educational attainment is based on an index, in which: less than basic = 1; basic = 2; general or special secondary = 3; and tertiary = 4.

els of poverty—presumably because open unemployment is a luxury enjoyed only by the residents of Dushanbe.

Rural location, on the other hand, is strongly associated with high levels of regional poverty in Bulgaria and Romania, and more weakly, in Russia, Turkey and the two Central Asian countries. In Poland, the relationship is reversed: rural regions have lower levels of poverty. Low levels of education are associated with poverty in Romania and Turkey, but not in Poland or Bulgaria. Large household size is strongly associated with poverty in Romania and Turkey, but not in Poland or Tajikistan.

The absence of a consistent statistical relationship between regional poverty and these four other regional characteristics does not suggest that the relationship does not exist. There are two reasons. First, the geographical units used in the analysis are too large. Variations that would affect individual job markets (commuter sheds) are subsumed in the regional averages. At the NUTS2 level, for example, the region encompassing Warsaw is 33 percent rural. The impact of scale on the apparent relationship between regional characteristics is illustrated by the comparison of results for Bulgaria shown in Table 3. Using a finer (NUTS3) level of analysis reverses the sign of the correlation coefficient for unemployment and virtually eliminates the correlation between rural location and poverty.

Second, poverty has different causes in different places. In Poland, for example, poverty in the western regions is associated with the collapse of collectivized agriculture. The western regions were annexed by Poland after the Second World War. Land formerly in private ownership was converted into large state farms. These were restructured at the beginning of the 1990s. Most state farm laborers—uneducated and unprepared to seek work in the market economy—lost their jobs. Many remain unemployed. In the east, agriculture was dominated by small farms which remained in private ownership throughout the socialist period. There, poverty is associated with an absence of urban job opportunities. (Several of the traditional urban centers of these regions—Vilnius and Lvov—now lie across international boundaries.) According to the recent World Bank report (2004c) on regional policy in Poland, these areas are profoundly unattractive to manufacturing investors due to their remoteness from suppliers, unreliable infrastructure, absence of business support services, and well-educated skilled staff, and poor living conditions for managerial staff.

What does this imply for regional development—for using the creation of higher-wage employment opportunities as a solution to poverty in poor regions? Two of the Poverty Report's four explanatory factors are clearly "people" characteristics: educational attainment and household size. Thus to some degree, poverty is caused by labor force characteristics—low levels of education—and large families. The significance of unemployment, however, is difficult to interpret. On one hand it may represent a locational characteristic: a large labor force actively looking for work and ready to take it if employment opportunities existed. Or it may represent a "people" characteristic: a labor force too unproductive to be attractive to potential employers. By the same token, the significance of rural location is ambiguous. While the term might be interpreted to mean "too remote to take advantage of non-farm employment opportunities in other regions" it might also mean "too unskilled to do so."

If high levels of regional poverty are explained by high levels of unemployment or a predominance of low productivity employment, then there may be a case for encouraging the growth of better job opportunities in such regions. However, much of the economic literature on regional development suggests that such efforts should be undertaken cautiously.

CHAPTER 3

The Market Approach

Geography does not feature prominently in the conventional economic development literature. This instead emphasizes policies at the national level—fiscal discipline, trade liberalization (including competitive exchange rates and the relaxation of FDI controls), tax reform (to lower marginal rates and broaden the tax base), interest rate liberalization, and the redirection of public expenditure toward sectors (such as infrastructure, education, and health) offering both high economic returns and the potential to improve income distribution (Williamson 2000). This non-spatial approach is reiterated in the Bank's work on private sector development, which emphasizes straightforward and consistently administered business regulation, property rights, and the development of the financial sector to provide access to credit as key factors in the development of private businesses.

From this perspective, the primary role of government is to make good macro policies and let the geographical chips fall where they may. "Regional policy" would be largely confined to the removal of impediments to labor and capital flows. This might include the abolition of nationally uniform minimum wages and industry-wide collective bargaining practices, so that firms have an incentive to invest in locations with cheap but productive labor. It might include cuts in unemployment benefits and other forms of social protection to encourage working-age people in lagging regions to migrate. It might also include housing policy reforms (including the abolition of rent control) to increase the supply of housing in potential destinations. However, it would not include direct government involvement in the location decisions of firms or labor.

Under these conditions, it is argued, capital and labor, free of impediments, will move to the locations where their respective returns are highest. Capital will move in pursuit of higher returns. Labor will move in pursuit of higher wages. And because returns to capital and labor reflect their respective productivity, the result will be an economy that is geographically efficient. Geographic concentrations of poverty—poverty traps—will also diminish, as labor in economically backward regions moves to more promising locations in search of higher wages.

This view is reinforced by the literature on economic geography. The literature identifies a range of factors (wage costs, capital costs, costs of inputs, and so forth) which affect the size and productivity of a regional economy. Some of these are amenable to policy influence. But the literature suggests that fixed geographical attributes (referred to as "first nature" or "first advantage" in the recent literature) reinforced by agglomeration economies are the key determinants of the location of economic activity. This suggests that efforts to thwart the dictates of economic geography are likely to be ineffective or costly.

The prevailing theory of regional growth is based on a Keynesian model. This emphasizes the competitiveness of a region's exports as the main determinant of growth (Armstrong and Taylor 2000). Once established, external demand for the product in which the region is specialized will partly determine its subsequent growth. External demand will, in turn, depend upon aggregate demand for the product in which the region specializes, as well as the region's continuing competitiveness in the production of that product (Hanson 2000; Fujita and Thiesse 2002).

One assumption of the early versions of this model was that the initial stimulus to a region's economic development arises from its access to natural resources. The Heckscher-Ohlin theorem, for example, argued regions will have a comparative advantage in the production of commodities that use their relatively abundant factors intensively. This is now recognized as insufficient. Natural resources are not the sole explanation for a region's comparative advantage. Burgess and Venables (2004) have proposed a broader definition of the initial stimulus for growth which "refers to the conditions needed to provide an environment in which new activities can be profitably developed, such as favorable access to inputs, access to markets, basic infrastructure, and an "appropriate" institutional environment."

One factor on which there is no disagreement is the importance of agglomeration economies in sustaining the growth of particular regions. Such economies may accrue at the level of an individual plant, where large scale permits a more efficient use of capital equipment. They may accrue at the industry level, where access to a common pool of specialized suppliers and appropriately-skilled labor provides advantages to firms located near large concentrations of other firms in their own industry. (The larger the pool of workers that a firm can access, the more likely it is to be able find the exact skills that suit its needs; Venables 2006). Or they may occur at the regional or city level, where location in an area with a varied economy gives firms ready access to non-specialized services (such as financial and legal services) and large consumer markets. Prominent economists differ over the relative importance of these three forms of agglomeration economies. Paul Krugman (2000), an early advocate of the so-called "new economic geography," argues that the first and third of these factors are most important. In his view, scale economies at the plant level will prompt firms to produce in a single location. The need to minimize transport costs will prompt them to locate near large consumer markets. Thus, firms will tend to locate in large cities in order to maximize scale economies and minimize transport costs. Michael Porter (2000) puts more emphasis on the second factor, arguing that intra-industry agglomeration economies will tend to cause firms in the same sector to cluster together, while permitting different regions to specialize in different sectors. Neither disputes the overriding impact of agglomeration economies on the location economic activity. Rosenthal and Strange's (2004) survey of the literature attempts to quantify the impact of agglomeration economies. They conclude that doubling city size increases factor productivity by 3–8 percent. Thus, moving from a city of 50,000 inhabitants to one of five million increases productivity by more than 50 percent.

This process is self-reinforcing—up to a point. As plants increase in scale, their production costs will continue to fall. As firms in the same sector continue to congregate, their cost advantage over rivals in other regions will increase. As the consumer market grows, activities that require large consumer markets to operate profitably will find the region increasingly attractive. The increased diversification of the region's economy will in turn increase the region's propensity to consume locally, reducing import leakage and stimulating local growth (Hanson 2000; Fujita and Thiesse 2002).

Some of the literature argues that this process will eventually reverse itself. As regions increase in population, diseconomies of agglomeration will set in. Transportation costs will rise. Housing prices will increase, forcing firms to pay higher wages. At the same time, the benefits of agglomeration may peak, at least for some industries. According to the product cycle theory, agglomeration economies will be most important when production technologies are new and firms require ready access to late-breaking innovations and specialized suppliers. As technology matures and production becomes routinized, the importance of these factors will decline. Firms will then disperse to take advantage of lower land and labor costs in outlying areas. On the other hand, if firms are highly dependent on a network of suppliers or on capabilities embodied in the local labor force, it is unlikely the sector will relocate (Venables 2006).

This does not imply that capital will flood into lagging regions, however. The factors that motivated a firm's initial location decisions will determine its subsequent moves. If access to skilled labor is important, firms may move to locations where skilled labor is cheaper, but not where it is unavailable. As a result, some development economists[11] have argued that agglomeration economies, in an environment of mobile labor and capital markets, will result in ever-increasing inequality among regions.[12]

The empirical evidence seems to bear this out. Rates of regional convergence have been very slow in industrial countries Sala-i-Martin's review (1996) of five European countries, the United States, and Japan show that regions tend to converge at a rate of two percent per year. More recent data for Western European countries suggests that regional economic disparities (as measured by GRP per capita) have scarcely budged over the last nine years, in spite of the efforts of the EU (as described below). As shown in Chart 3, the coefficients of variation for France, Spain, and Germany barely moved over the period 1995–2003. While regional disparities in Italy diminished, those in the UK increased.

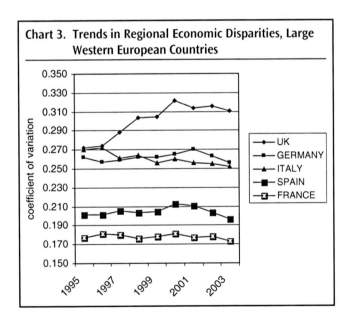

Chart 3. Trends in Regional Economic Disparities, Large Western European Countries

---

11. Dating back at least as far as Myrdal (1957).

12. *Regional Cohesion Evidence and Theories of Regional Growth and Convergence,* Center for Economic Policy Research, Discussion Paper 1075, London, UK.

CHAPTER 4

The Case for Intervention

The market-based approach to regional development has its critics. They argue that labor and capital markets will not, on their own, produce a satisfactory geographical outcome; that even if policy-induced barriers to migration were removed, people in poor regions would not migrate (at least not in sufficient numbers). They also argue that private capital markets will not ferret out all high-return investments. Such critics see a more active role for the public sector in determining the location of economic activity.

Labor Market Failures

Classical economic migration theory suggests that wage differentials among regions (or expected differentials at a future time) will prompt people to move from low-wage to high-wage regions (Lucas 2002). Internal migration did increase sharply in a number of ECA countries at the beginning of the transition. However, this may have been a one-time phenomenon. Much of the spike in migration in CIS countries appears to have been driven by "diaspora migration"—the return of people to their ethnic homelands—and the movement of workers away from peripheral areas that had been assigned to them by the Soviet central planners. For example, more than one million people relocated from Siberia and the Russian North and Far East to the more central parts of Russia. This represented about 12 percent of the populations of these areas. Russian census takers discovered nearly 13,000 ghost towns in peripheral regions, where cities that had once existed had become fully depopulated and another 35,000 where the population had dwindled to ten or fewer people. According to the World Bank's recent Jobs Report, these two effects appear to have run their course. Consequently, migration has slowed despite persistent income and quality of

21

life differentials (World Bank 2005a). This finding is borne out by the figures cited in the recent World Bank paper (2006) on labor mobility in the new member states of the EU. As shown in Chart 4, internal migration in Poland, Slovakia, and the Czech Republic represents less than 0.5 percent of the working population in those countries as opposed to 1.5 percent in Germany, and nearly 2.5 percent in France, Netherlands, and the UK.[13] The study concludes that internal migration is ineffective in reducing regional disparities in the new member states and candidate countries.[14]

Why don't people—at least working age people—in economically depressed regions move? To begin with, they have good economic reasons not to do so: in many cases they would be no better off if they did. Harris and Todaro (1970) noted long ago that the propensity to migrate is determined not by wage differentials alone but by wage differentials adjusted by likelihood of obtaining work. Even rich regions in ECA countries have high rates of unemployment. In Romania, for example, the rate of open unemployment in the Bucharest region was ten percent (in 2004). In Poland, the rate in the region encompassing Warsaw was 14.6 percent. Although these rates are sometimes lower than in poorer regions (especially in countries with dispersed manufacturing or generous social safety nets), they still suggest that migration to a rich region does not guarantee a high-paying job. In some Central Asian countries, non-agricultural employment opportunities have virtually disappeared. In the Kyrgyz Republic, the proportion of the labor force employed in manufacturing fell by 17 percentage points during the transition. As the services sector failed to expand proportionately, employment in agriculture increased to 20 percent of the labor force.

Dim employment prospects particularly affect potential migrants from poor areas as they lack qualifications for the sorts of jobs available in more prosperous regions. Since the transition, the skill content of employment has shifted upward. Labor demand now tends to be concentrated on higher-skilled positions. The World Bank Jobs Report notes that job growth since the transition has been concentrated in the service sector in urban regions, and these jobs may require skills not available to unemployed blue collar workers in other regions. In Bulgaria and Lithuania, for example, more than 20 percent of the unemployed fail to find jobs because their skills fall short of employer requirements (World Bank 2005a). This is a particular problem in one-industry manufacturing towns, where the majority of the population acquired skills highly specific to that industry.

Liquidity constraints also inhibit migration. Relocation costs are non-trivial and may be beyond the means of potential migrants in poor regions—raising the ironic prospect that rising incomes in a lagging region provide potential migrants with the wherewithal to relocate just as the incentive to do so vanishes. Andrienko and Guriev (2004) estimate that one-third of Russian regions are locked in poverty traps merely because residents lack the wherewithal to finance a move to more prosperous regions. Liquidity constraints particularly affect rural areas, where uncertain land title prevents potential migrants from converting their assets into a form (cash) they can use on arrival.

Government policies may also unintentionally discourage migration by making it more comfortable to stay home. Extensive unemployment benefits and social assistance reduce the pressure to migrate from declining regions. According to the recent Bank Jobs

---

13. Gross regional outflow is the percentage of the working-age population relocating to other regions within the country in a given year.

14. Fdrmuc (2004) and Ederveen and Bardsley (2004), respectively, cited by Huber (2006).

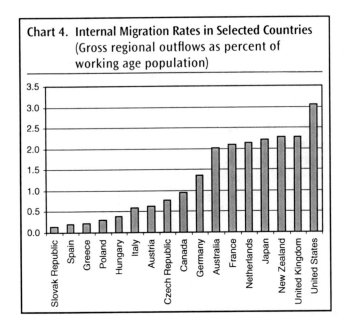

Chart 4. Internal Migration Rates in Selected Countries (Gross regional outflows as percent of working age population)

Report (World Bank 2005a), "social benefits have provided disincentives for migration, especially at an early stage in the transition." Under Poland's system of unemployment insurance, for example, qualified workers receive benefits (equal to 80 percent to 120 percent of the base benefit, depending on length of service) for periods ranging from six months in regions with low unemployment to 18 months in regions of high unemployment. In addition, unemployed workers close to retirement age receive pre-retirement benefits linked to their pensions. In the past, disability pensions have also been used as a form of long-term unemployment benefit. (Rules for eligibility were made more stringent in 1998.) Low-income households are also eligible for a guaranteed temporary social assistance benefit. The Living Standards Assessment for Poland (World Bank 2004a) argues that these benefits are a principal cause of low labor mobility.

Housing policies may also discourage migration. During the transition, flats were typically transferred to their occupants at little or no cost. As a result, the cost of remaining in one's own flat is relatively low. At the same, housing policies—such as rent control—have discouraged new construction, driving up the cost of housing in regions that are expanding economically. An OECD study (2002) of the Czech Republic found that a heavily regulated rental housing market has inhibited labor mobility by creating substantial price differentials between regions. (A large share of inter-regional migration occurs only because the persons involved exchange their apartments; Feldman 2004.) According to the recent Bank Jobs Report (World Bank 2005a), the costs of renting a studio apartment in Warsaw is equal to 70 percent of the average monthly net wage of a less-skilled worker.

It has been argued that nationally uniform minimum wages and collective bargaining arrangements discourage migration by sustaining artificially high wage rates in poor regions. But this presumes that: (i) minimum wage levels are high enough to affect actual wages; and (ii) the workers benefiting from these practices are able to keep their jobs. There is some evidence for the former. In Poland, for example, in regions with high unemployment rates, the average minimum wage is over 90 percent of the actual wage of workers at the lower end of the wage distribution. One might expect that firms that are forced to pay artificially high wages in poor regions would relocate to more prosperous regions where wages better reflect labor productivity. This would increase the unemployment rate in poor regions, and as such, provide an impetus for out-migration. Rather than being motivated by low wages, migrant workers would be motivated by high unemployment. There is some evidence for this. Feldman's study in the Visegrad countries, for example, finds that the Poland's relatively high and nationally uniform minimum wage has increased unemployment in recent years, particularly in relatively poor regions. (These effects did not appear in Hungary or the Czech Republic because minimum wages in those countries are relatively low.) National wage setting therefore appears to inhibit outmigration only where workers are unlikely to be dismissed (as in the case of state-owned enterprises).

Over and above strict economic calculations, migration is inhibited by psychological costs. Gravity models of migration show that the propensity to migrate declines as the distance between the origin and the destination increases. This suggests that potential migrants attach considerable significance to the costs and risks associated with migration (Lucas 2002). Feldman (2004) attributes the low rates of inter-regional migration in the Czech Republic, Hungary and Poland to the "attitudes and habits of people." In a 1999 survey conducted in the Czech Republic, 66.3 percent of respondents who were currently unemployed said they were not willing to move for the sake of a job. He attributes this to the traditionally close system of family ties, which were reinforced during the era of central planning, when job assignments were virtually permanent and few people were required to move. For ethnic minorities, migration may also be inhibited by fears of discrimination in destination regions.

The failure of migration to eliminate poverty traps does not, of course, call for a strategy based solely on bringing jobs to lagging regions. Governments can also remove impediments to migration. Labor market liberalization can increase employment opportunities in potential destination regions. Reductions in unemployment benefits and social assistance (for the working age population) can increase pressure to move. Housing market reforms can reduce the cost of housing in destination regions. Rural land adjudication can provide potential migrants with a stake to finance the costs of relocation. Investments in human capital—on education and skills training—can also increase the likelihood that people in poor regions have access to better paying jobs once they migrate. Yet, the carrot of better paying jobs and the stick of reduced benefits may not be sufficient to eliminate poverty traps entirely, particularly within the time frame confronting many governments in the ECA region.

Capital Market Failures

Critics of the market-based approach to regional development also point to failures in the capital market. In the ECA region, access to credit is a widespread constraint to firms' ability to invest and create new jobs. According to the Bank's recent Jobs Report (World Bank 2005a), access to finance stands out as the most important determinant of private sector employment in the region. There is little evidence that capital flows are serving to reduce disparities in regional economic development.

Flows of FDI have largely remained concentrated in capital cities and other centers of economic activity, along with regions close to western European borders. In Russia, close to 60 percent of FDI has gone to Moscow City, Moscow oblast, St. Petersburg City and Leningrad oblast, while other units of the federation generally received no more than two percent of the total. In the Slovak Republic, 60 percent of all foreign investment is clustered in the Bratislava region. In Poland, 50 percent of the initial capital of enterprises with foreign participation is concentrated in the region encompassing Warsaw. Using regional data covering the 1993 to 1998 period, Cieslik[15] found that regional unemployment rates are negatively correlated with

---

15. Cited in World Bank (2006).

foreign investment, that is, that foreign investors favor regions that are already booming. In Hungary, a recent study of foreign (and domestic) firms over the 1993–2000 period concluded that firms are not moving to high unemployment regions despite the relative scarcity of skilled workers in more dynamic regions. However, the concentration of FDI in capital cities is not, *ipso facto*, an indicator of market failure. The Hungary study, for example, found investment returns were higher in dynamic regions as the high productivity of labor in such regions more than compensates for the higher wages there.

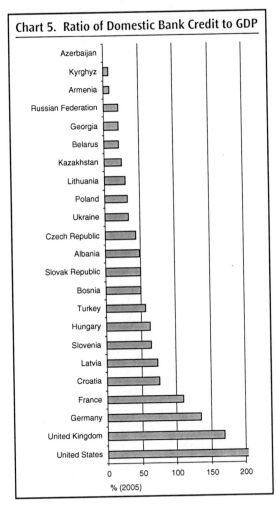

Chart 5. Ratio of Domestic Bank Credit to GDP

Investment financing from the domestic private sector is limited in most of the ECA region. The private financial sector in the ECA region (with the exception of Turkey) was severely under-developed at the dawn of the 1990s. Credit directed by central planning bodies was the only source of financing for enterprises. Equity and corporate bond markets did not exist. The financial sector has since undergone a major transformation. Most of the former socialist countries have privatized the vast majority of their banks, and most banking systems are majority-private in total credit, assets, deposits, and capital. As a result, government ownership in the banking system has declined in most of the region. Based on 2001 EBRD data, only seven countries (Albania, Azerbaijan, Belarus, Bosnia-Herzegovina, Turkmenistan, Uzbekistan, and Yugoslavia) still had banking systems with a majority of assets in state hands and several of these were moving ahead with privatization and liquidation that will change these figures. Only Azerbaijan, Belarus, Turkmenistan, and Uzbekistan were expected to have a majority of assets in state banks by end 2002. In recent years, domestic credit has expanded rapidly in the higher income EU accession countries. In Croatia, it is now equivalent to 76 percent of GDP; in Latvia, 73 percent. But elsewhere, domestic credit remains limited. In the region as a whole, it averages 32 percent of GDP, as opposed to 170 percent of GDP in high income OECD countries. As shown in Chart 5, in Russia, it is 21 percent of GDP; in the Kyrgyz Republic, only eight percent (World Bank 2007a).[16]

---

16. Figures for ECA exclude Moldova, Tajikistan, Turkmenistan, and Uzbekistan, where data is not available.

Reform efforts in the financial sector are now focused on governance and the intro-duction of safe asset management practices. Under these circumstances, the supply of credit for long-term investment in plant and equipment will continue to be severely constrained. Privatized banks show a strong preference for holding assets in the form of high yield gov-ernment bonds rather than encountering risks associated with private sector lending. Where banks do provide commercial lending, they tend to focus on less risky short term working capital rather than longer term investment.

Whether domestic financial institutions, once consolidated, will be more willing than their foreign counterparts to ferret out investment opportunities in lagging regions remains to be seen. Armstrong and Taylor (2000) argue that domestic financial sector development is likely to have the opposite effect. In their view, credit shortages in depressed regions will become particularly severe once the financial sector is integrated, since it will be easier for capital to flow to regions where confidence is high.

Coordination Failures

The most telling flaw in the market-based approach to regional development is its failure to address coordination failures—the need for different economic actors to coordinate their activities if any one of them is to be viable. As put by Rodrik (2004):

> An individual orchid producer contemplating whether to invest in a greenhouse needs to know that there is an electrical grid he can access nearby, that logistics and transport networks are in place, that quarantine measures have been taken to protect his plants, and that his country has been marketed abroad as a dependable supplier of high quality orchids. All of these services have high fixed costs and are unlikely to be provided by individual private companies unless they have an assurance that there will be enough greenhouses to demand their services in the first place.

Coordination failures affect both the private and public sectors. Public infrastructure investments in remote regions will not pay off unless households and firms are present to use them (and have the wherewithal to do so). Yet, firms may not locate to such regions unless infrastructure is already present. By the same token, assembly plants may not locate in remote regions unless local suppliers are available. Local suppliers will not emerge unless a customer for their products is within reach. The problem of coordination failures has been used to justify a prominent role for the public sector in coordinating the investment and production decisions of different entrepreneurs. Their record is reviewed below.

Box 4. Clusters

Some governments have attempted to address certain coordination failures by encouraging the formation of clusters. This approach, popularized by Michael Porter, is predicated on the notion that governments can create industry-level agglomeration economies by encouraging firms in related sectors to locate in the same place at the same time. While the site in question might not be viable for any firm acting in isolation, clustering permits them to benefit from reduced transportation costs and shared access to specialized services. In theory, it permits producers of finished products to have day-to-day contact with their suppliers, and suppliers of intermediate goods to have day-to-day contact with their consumers.

There is some empirical evidence for the positive effect of clustering. Henderson (1997), in his work on the United States, found that firms, particularly in the technology sectors, grew fastest when there was a concentration of firms in the same county. His subsequent analysis (Henderson 2003) showed that plants located in sectoral clusters (concentrations of plants in the same sector in the same county) had higher productivity, particularly if they were independent (non-branch) plants.

The cluster approach is not without its critics. Martin and Sunley (2003) argue that the concept is too vague to be operational. They note that "much of the evidence used in support of (clustering) is anecdotal and based on success stories about particular locations." One of the few detailed studies that exist (of metalworking across the United States) found no evidence that clustered firms adopt new technologies more rapidly than their more geographically-dispersed or isolated counterparts (Harrison and others 1996). Similarly, Catherine Beaudry's study (2000) of the impact of clusters on firm growth and innovation for a range of industries across Europe found the results to be ambivalent. A recent study of Ireland's competitiveness by O'Malley and Egeraat found that despite "a scarcity of Porter-style indigenous clusters, Irish indigenous industry has performed well through the 1990s."[17]

But the key question for this report is whether governments can bring clusters into being—and whether such clusters can be induced to form in lagging regions. A recent Brookings Institution report (Cortright 2006) suggests that this may be difficult. It argues that entrepreneurs start clusters and do so on the basis of prior experience and interests, building on local contacts and business knowledge. As a result, "independent but complementary decisions by a range of economic actors all converge to reinforce growth in initially successful places." Rosenthal and Strange's work on the New York region confirms this view. They found that new firms tend to locate in areas where their own sector is already concentrated. (Although other studies of the New York region have found that new firms tend to be slightly more decentralized than older firms in the sector, such firms tended to have a higher death rate.) Cortright, similarly, argues that regional specialization tends to persist over time, suggesting that regions with an industry concentration will be best positioned to increase it, and conversely, that those without a particular concentration will find it difficult to create one, either indigenously or by attracting firms from other locations. He argues that opportunities to dramatically change the concentration of particular industries hinge on dramatic shifts in industrial structure or technology and that "despite a handful of instances in which public policy avowedly set out to change a region's economic base (Research Triangle Park in North Carolina is frequently cited) failures are far more common" (Cortright 2006). Krugman, for his part, discounts the role of government policy, asserting that "small accidental events start a cumulative process in which the presence of a large number of firms and workers acts as an incentive for still more firms and workers to congregate in a particular location. The resulting pattern may be determined by underlying resources and technology at some very aggregate level, but at ground level there is a striking role for history and accident."[18]

Cortright concludes that clusters are best viewed as an organizing principle for economic development—a useful framework for understanding a regional economy and perhaps a way of identifying groups to work with. He adds that working with groups of firms in the same cluster can also be helpful by shifting the focus of discussion from firm-level rent seeking (subsidies, tax breaks) to more widely shared competitive problems.

---

17. O'Malley and Egeraat (2000), cited in Cambridge Econometrics (2002).
18. Paul Krugman, cited in Cortright (2006).

CHAPTER 5

Policy Instruments

Government efforts to manipulate the location of economic activity have a long and checkered history. They include outright prohibitions on the location of new factories in "overdeveloped" areas—an example is the British Government's prohibition on new factories in Greater London in the 1920s. They include credit subsidies and tax incentives to firms locating in areas where growth is desired. They also include more indirect inducements—the provision of off-site infrastructure or worker training, regional marketing or branding efforts, assistance with land acquisition and in overcoming regulatory hurdles, and urban renewal projects aimed at making lagging cities more attractive to managers and highly skilled professionals.

Macro Level Infrastructure

Building macro-level infrastructure—power and telecommunications lines, highways, railroads, port and airport facilities, and even water and sewer utilities—in depressed regions is a time-honored approach to regional development. The 2005 OECD report, *Building Competitive Regions,* notes that "the expectation that improvements in physical infrastructure will generate productivity gains for local business and increase the attractiveness of an area for investment has been a recurring theme in OECD reviews of specific regions." The report further argues that the "(OECD) work across a range of regions demonstrates that the presence of efficient physical infrastructure and related services are the key to economic development."

However, the impact of infrastructure investment has been difficult to quantify. There have been many attempts to demonstrate a statistical relationship between infrastructure and economic growth in the development literature. Many such studies show very high returns

---

Box 5. Implicit Regional Policies

It should be noted at the outset that explicit regional policies can be overwhelmed by policies that have no explicit regional objective but have large and disparate impacts on different regions within a country. In the United States, for example, military spending has had an important influence on the geography of economic growth. Since World War II, procurement in the aircraft, communication, computing, and electronics industries have helped seed new government-oriented industrial complexes in Los Angeles, Seattle, and Silicon Valley (Marcusen 1995). In Europe, similarly, the reduction in trade barriers that accompanied EU accession benefited some regions more than others. There is substantial evidence that in the new EU member states and candidate countries, western border regions benefited disproportionately from cross-border shopping from EU-15 countries, foreign direct investment, and higher trade exposure. As a result, they experienced lower unemployment rates and higher GDP growth, particularly in the earlier years of the transition (Huber 2006).[19] The EU's Common Agricultural Policy (CAP) has also had an effect on the geography of growth in Europe. The Sapir report (2003) argues that the redistributive impact of Structural Funds—the negative correlation between the amount of Structural Funds a region receives and its GRP per capita—is entirely offset by the CAP transfers and other internal programs.

---

on a time-series basis. Some cross-national studies, using public investments in transport and communications, or stocks in roads, railways, and telephones, show that infrastructure variables are positively and significantly correlated with growth (World Bank 1994). In both types of studies, however, it is not clear whether infrastructure investment causes growth or growth causes infrastructure investment. Early work on the subject by Aschauer (1989) produced high and positive elasticities of national and regional output with respect to public capital. His well-known "crowding in" study purports to demonstrate that virtually any investment in infrastructure will increase productivity. Yet, as Button (2002) points out, Aschauer's work merely demonstrates a correlation between infrastructure and productivity. It does not demonstrate causation. Regions with highly productive labor forces may have high levels of infrastructure because they can afford them, not because they need them.

In the ECA region, empirical evidence suggests that EU Structural Funds have clearly spurred a great deal of activity. During the 1994–1999 programming period, Objective 1 structural funds financed the construction or upgrading of 4,104 km of highways and 31,844 km of other roads. This construction had at least a short-term Keynesian effect, giving a temporary boost to the local economy through the expenditure of funds from outside the region (Bradley 2005). Although some of this impact was offset by the use of imported labor and materials, Martin (2003) argues that "the construction of a highway increase(d) the local demand for goods and labor and hence increase(d) the incomes available in the region."

Whether this investment has had a sustained impact on growth or productivity in the regions where it was concentrated is not clear. There have been several attempts to analyze the impact of EU-financed infrastructure investments on regional economic growth using econometric techniques.[20] Basile, de Nardis, and Girardi (2004) analyzed the evidence from

---

19. Note that governments often use regional development programs to offset the unintended spatial impact of non-spatial policies.

20. A survey of macroeconomic models regional economic disparities is available in Herve (2000).

the late 1980s to the late 1990s for twelve countries in the EU, and were unable to find strong evidence of regional convergence of real per capita income, labor productivity, or employment rates, despite the "massive allocation of Structural Funds" to poorer jurisdictions. Stierle's survey (2004) of the econometric evidence on the impact of EU regional transfers on regional economic growth finds that "a few studies find a positive impact from Structural Funds while others do not." He notes, however, that most of these attempts to link national and regional GDP or productivity growth to cohesion assistance by econometric regressions are "plagued with methodological, econometric, and data weaknesses." Cappelen (2003), similarly, is highly critical of existing econometric studies, arguing that the conclusions of these models depend more on the hypotheses underlying them than on any empirical evidence.

Non-econometric policy reviews have also failed to find a systematic relationship between EU structural fund allocations and regional economic growth. A report (ECOTEC n.d.) for the European Commission on the impact of structural funds in the 1994–1999 plan period concluded: "interregional disparities remain and for some regions the position does not appear to have progressed significantly . . . (T)his raises some questions as to the ability of Objective 1 to support balanced territorial development." The 2003 Sapir report, similarly, concludes that "it is not possible to establish conclusively what the relative performance of these regions would have been in the absence of EU cohesion policies." Boldrin and Canova (2003) note that regional convergence within individual member states of the EU came to a virtual halt just after the structural and cohesion policies were introduced.[21]

The failure of these studies to find a systematic relationship between EU-funded infrastructure investment and regional growth does not mean that the relationship does not exist. To varying degrees, all the studies suffer from two flaws. First, they treat all infrastructure investment as equivalent: the construction of an industrial park in a remote region is given the same weight as the completion of a vital link in the national highway network. But all infrastructure investment is not equivalent. Economic rates of return vary. As described in Box 6, even similar investments can have very different impacts depending on the conditions in the region in which they are constructed.

Second, the studies (to varying degrees) fail to account for the range of other factors that affect rates of growth or convergence. EU-funded infrastructure investments are clearly not the only factor affecting the economies of specific regions. As noted earlier, changes in trade regimes or sectoral policies have an impact. Changes in external demand for the region's exports do too. Most of the studies reviewed for this report do not isolate the impact of infrastructure investments from these contemporaneous influences. As a result, as Stierle (2004) concludes, "no causality can be inferred from. . . . the lack of convergence or from its speed, which may result from many economic, social and policy factors other than the EU assistance." In a more positive light, the Sapir report (2003) concludes that "efforts by the EU through the Structural Funds and the Cohesion Fund to promote convergence can only be a complement to other factors. They must be accompanied by national policies to put in place a favorable a favorable environment for investment and for human capital formation."

---

21. Note that disparities among *the individual member states* of the EU narrowed during this period.

Box 6. Transportation Investments are a Two-Edged Sword

Empirical evidence suggests that some forms of infrastructure investment can be a two edged sword—particularly in the case of transport infrastructure. Investments in *intra*-regional transportation infrastructure can facilitate agglomeration economies by reducing the costs of transport within the region. However, investments that facilitate interregional trade can adversely affect firms in poorer regions by reducing the price of goods imported from elsewhere. In effect, such improvements are equivalent to reducing tariffs on international trade. While such improvements benefit the national economy as a whole (and consumers in poor regions in particular) they adversely affect local producers by undercutting prices (Faini 1983; World Bank 2000). In effect, such investments encourage firms to relocate to richer regions as this enables them to reap the benefits of increasing returns to scale in the richer market while facilitating sales to the poorer one (Martin 1998). This is borne out in a study by Combes and Lafourcade,[22] which suggests that the drop in transportation costs in France over the past 20 years has resulted in a decreased concentration around the Paris region to the benefit of other major cities but to the detriment of the surrounding poorer jurisdictions. Similar studies in Italy suggest that the construction of highways between north and south may have led not to convergence, but to the relative decline of the south (Faini 1983). Ironically, the recent Bank report on migration recommends building more highways so that people can work in places where the jobs are without having to change residences.

Some of the recent literature does attempt to distinguish the circumstances under which infrastructure investments are likely to have an impact. A recent survey by de la Fuente (2003) concludes that "there are sufficient indications that public infrastructure investments contribute significantly to productivity growth, at least in regions where a saturation point has not been reached. The returns are quite high when infrastructure is scarce and basic networks have not been completed but fall sharply thereafter." A similar conclusion is reached by Canning and Pedroni (1999) who find high returns to investment when infrastructure is scarce and basic networks have not been completed, but sharply falling returns thereafter. The 1994 *World Development Report* concluded that "the economic impact of infrastructure investment depends on whether it provides the kind of services valued by users, which in turn depends on such characteristics as quality and reliability, as well as on quantity. Matching supply to what is demanded is what is essential." The same admonition would appear to apply to investment in lagging regions.

Overall, this suggests that not all infrastructure investments are likely to have a positive impact on regional economic growth. An industrial park in a remote and desolate part of the country is unlikely to stimulate the local economy. It does suggest, however, that the right sort of infrastructure investment can provide a necessary, if not sufficient, condition for economic growth. What is important is to identify such investments. Methodologies for capital investment planning are discussed in Chapter 7.

---

22. P. Combes and M. Lafourcade, "Transportation Costs Decline and Regional Inequalities: Evidence from France," *CEPR Discussion Paper 2894* (1978–1993).

Table 4. Statistical Relationship Between Educational Attainment and Deep Poverty Rates

| | Educational attainment* | | |
	Mean	Coefficient of variation	Correlation with poverty rate
Poland	2.77	.022	−.12
Bulgaria	2.97	.087	.05
Romania	2.54	.061	−.91
Russia	3.18	.024	−.29
Turkey	2.05	.062	−.83
Kazakhstan	3.32	.102	−.33
Tajikistan	2.80	.051	−.06

*based on an index, in which: less than basic = 1; basic = 2; general or special secondary = 3; and tertiary = 4.

Education and Training

Education, by enhancing skills, productivity, and adaptability, is said to be conducive to long-term economic growth (Lucas 1988). Other things being equal, this might suggest that investment in education would be an effective means of stimulating growth in poorer regions. But several caveats are in order. First, education does not increase labor productivity if there are no jobs requiring it. Education increases only the supply side of a broader equation: it increases the availability of skilled labor but not the demand for it. In the absence of policies that increase the demand for labor, increased opportunities for education can translate into a highly skilled but unemployed population. Recent Bank work found that some developing countries have expanded education only to see rising subsequent unemployment rates and falling returns. In other countries, the highly educated find work only in the public sector, where their productivity is questionable (Vandycke 2001).

Second, the education that is provided must be relevant to the market place. There is increasing evidence that the sort of education offered in the Soviet era is no longer relevant to the labor market. According to the recent Bank Jobs Report (World Bank 2005a), skill deficiencies are a significant obstacle to firm growth, especially in the Central and Eastern European countries, where restructuring has proceeded at a higher speed. In the Czech Republic, Hungary, Latvia, and Poland, 35 to 40 percent of employers see the (lack of) skills of the available workforce as a significant obstacle to the growth of their firms. In Estonia, this proportion reaches 65 percent. Vocational education in Poland, for example, was traditionally organized along sectoral lines, with the pertinent ministry responsible for determining the vocational criteria. Schools normally focused on a single sector, and switching from one type of vocation to another was difficult. Similarly in Russia, many secondary institutions were directly linked to production enterprises. As long as enterprises remained unmodernized, there was also no need to update or modify training in the attached training institution. As a result, vocational training is often over-specialized and linked to jobs for which there is no longer any demand.

Finally, there is strong empirical evidence that education increases the propensity of people to move. A recent study of Russia, for example, found that many of the (prosperous) regions outside of central Russia are populated with newcomers who were educated elsewhere and who moved to the outlying regions in search of high paying jobs. Providing high-quality, market-relevant education in lagging regions is therefore likely to increase the incomes of those who receive it. But it may not benefit the economy of the region where it was provided.

Improving the Business Climate

Adverse business climates are another possible constraint on economic development in lagging regions. Recent Bank work (World Bank 2005a) analyzed constraints on the business environment among countries within the ECA region. These vary considerably among groups of countries. High taxes and strictly enforced labor regulations are a problem in the Central and Eastern European (CEE) and Southeastern European (SEE) countries. In the Czech Republic, Hungary, and Romania the tax wedge on labor use is around 50 percent. Labor regulations—including protections against dismissal—are demanding and are well-enforced. As a result, in the CEE, the proportion of firms complaining about labor regulations reaches as high as 30 percent and it is only slightly lower in the SEE countries. In the CIS countries, tax and labor regulation are often only weakly or selectively enforced and firms do not comply with them. (In the low-income CIS countries,[23] only ten percent of firms complain about labor regulations.) Nevertheless, the effort and risks required to evade these regulations add to the difficulties of starting and operating a business. A recent survey of start-up firms in Russia revealed that more than 90 percent of managers had to make extra-legal payments to secure government services or a business license. The firms that were most concerned about corruption invested 40 percent less than those that were least concerned about it (Johnson, McMillan, and Woodruff 2002). Other forms of regulation—business licensing (both initiation and renewal), customs and foreign exchange—are particularly burdensome for start-up businesses in many ECA countries. Access to serviced land has been cited as a constraint in some surveys. In the low income CIS countries, the judicial system is a constraint. Many businesses face unfair treatment, high costs, long delays, and weak enforcement in the courts. As a result, contracts can be, in effect, unenforceable. A survey of small manufacturing firms in Poland, Romania, Russia and Ukraine found that the perceived effectiveness of courts in resolving commercial disputes affected entrepreneurs' propensity to reinvest their profits (Johnson, McMillan, and Woodruff 2002).

The degree to which these constraints are particularly binding in the lagging regions of individual countries is not clear. In principle, legislation governing taxation, labor relations, and trade is fixed at the national level and is meant to apply uniformly throughout the country. (Locally-imposed and administered taxes are only a minor source of revenue in ECA countries.) Yet, administrative practices may vary among regions even when performed by officials of the central government. Tax administration is particularly susceptible to local discretion, in the form of disruptive and costly tax inspections, selective enforcement and associated extortion.

Some local governments have taken advantage of prevailing adverse business conditions by offering assistance in overcoming regulatory and bureaucratic obstacles as a means of attracting new investment. There is considerable anecdotal evidence of mayors interceding with the local offices of the national government to obtain favorable tax or regulatory treatment for favored firms or prospective investors. Mayors are also instrumental in assisting investors in land acquisition (a problem in many ex-socialist countries, where the status of land ownership is still in dispute; World Bank 2004b). This is clearly a second-best solution. First-best would be to address the adverse business conditions themselves by

---

23. Armenia, Azerbaijan, Georgia, the Kyrgyz Republic, Moldova, Tajikistan and Uzbekistan.

reducing regulatory burdens (in the CEE and SEE countries) and reducing administrative discretion and opportunities for corruption (in the CIS countries).

Firm-Specific Subsidies

Governments have employed a wide variety of explicit incentives to influence the location of economic growth. Traditionally, these have focused on influencing the movement of capital. Firm-specific subsidies (including tax relief and subsidized credit) have been the most common instruments. Such subsidies include the traditional firm-specific inducements for private investment: grants or soft loans to firms investing in favored regions, along with tax breaks (including reductions in both national and local taxes) and the provision of land and/or on-site infrastructure. They also include export processing zones, where firms are allowed duty-free access on all their imports (provided they export their outputs), exemptions from bureaucratic regulations and superior infrastructure and communications services.

This approach is being pursued, to varying degrees, throughout the ECA countries. The Czech Republic, for example, offers tax incentives along with the provision of low cost land and/or infrastructure (i.e., industrial zones) to eligible firms. While tax relief is available throughout the country, its size is differentiated by region, with the lowest proportion (20 percent) offered in Prague and higher proportions (46–50 percent) in the other regions of the country. Poland, similarly, offers an exemption from the income tax for firms located in 14 special economic zones.[24] In Turkey, according to the "Employment Encouragement in the Underdeveloped Regions" Law, enterprises operating in the 36 provinces with per capita GRPs below $1,500 (in 2001) are eligible for exemptions from the personal income tax and social insurance contributions normally required for newly hired employees. In Romania, firms located in the 28 officially designated disadvantaged zones are eligible for exemptions from profit taxes[25] and customs duties paid on imported raw materials and spare parts to be used in the production process. They are also eligible for financing programs financed from a Special Development Fund. Some Russian oblasts offer their own incentives. Samara Oblast Administration, for example, offers investment guarantees for new investment and tax credits for the development or re-equipment of existing factories.

There is a wide, but not very deep, literature on the impact of firm-specific subsidies on local economic development.[26] It is fairly unanimous in concluding that firms will, in

---

24. The exemption is based on either the volume of investment expenditure or on the number of new jobs created. Additional benefits for companies operating in special economic zones may be provided by local governments. These include exemptions from the real estate tax, assistance from the local employment offices in the training and recruitment of staff, and assistance with land acquisition.

25. For up to ten years, provided the exemption was granted before July 1, 2003.

26. This analysis focuses on the experience of Western Europe and North America and is based on the following articles, some of which include further reviews of the literature: Bradley (2005), Boldrin and Canova (2003), Cappelen and others (2003), ECOTEC (n.d.), Funck, Pizzati, and Burncko (2003), Garnier (2005), Hon and Fallon (2000), Martin (2003), OECD (2005), Shankar and Shah (2001), U.S. GAO (1996).

fact, locate in places where such incentives are available, provided the scale of incentives is sufficient. What is not agreed is:

- whether they will leave once the incentives expire;
- whether the investment will have a broader impact on the regional economy;
- whether the subsidy is the most cost-effective means of achieving the objective at hand; and

what the impact of any resulting relocation of economic activity will be on the efficiency of the economy as a whole and on the economies of regions where the activity might otherwise have located.

All of these issues are contentious. In principle, firm-specific location incentives are intended to be transitory, allowing firms to persevere until they achieve sufficient scale or overcome locational disadvantages such as remoteness from markets or suppliers. Under these circumstances, incentives enable firms to move to locations where long-run returns will be high but where the transitory costs discourage investment. How many firms survive the termination of their subsidies would appear to be an easily answered empirical question. It is not, however, revealed in the literature.

Firms brought in through incentives are expected to have broader impacts on the economy through purchases of inputs from local suppliers, sales of outputs to local producers, and through the impact of their employees' spending on local demand. The literature— particularly the reviews prepared for the Bank—argues that these expectations are often disappointed. Firms operate in isolation, importing equipment and materials from other regions and exporting their products outside the region. Similary, OECD (2005) reports that "numerous studies have found that . . . branch plants are weakly embedded in local production systems, generating very low levels of local supplier linkages."

Because incentives tend to be biased toward capital, they often have limited employment impacts. Employment impacts are further limited when the skills required by the new firm are not available locally. Under these circumstances, the firms have to import workers from outside the region. Some countries have attempted to counteract the bias against labor by imposing a ceiling on the amount of the incentive per job. Others have directly subsidized labor costs. In principle, labor subsidies encourage firms to substitute labor for capital, creating more jobs. However, critics have argued that such subsidies are not sustainable. Capital subsidies allow firms to re-equip and become competitive. Plants can graduate from capital subsidies. They never graduate from labor subsidies.

Subsidies can be expensive. In the early 1990s, South Carolina committed $70,000 per worker to obtain a BMW plant. Alabama spent over $200,000 per job to lure Mercedes. The indirect costs of subsidies may be even greater. Midelfart-Knarvik and Overman[27] found that regional policies in Europe have prompted firms to locate where they are less efficient, achieving the goal of dispersing economic activities, but at the cost of overall growth. As noted earlier, the Sapir report also found regional economic equalization to be incompatible with national economic growth.

---

27. Cited Funck, Pizzati, and Burncko (2003).

The U.S. literature emphasizes the costs of firm-specific incentives for neighboring jurisdictions. Locally-granted incentives are, in some cases, successful in luring new investment. Yet, evidence suggests that firms receiving such incentives merely relocate from other jurisdictions. While the incentives may stimulate growth in the jurisdiction that grants them, they stimulate no growth in the economy as a whole. Some U.S. studies suggest that firms use the threat of relocation merely to induce additional subsidies from the jurisdictions in which they are currently located. In response, the Economic Development Administration has had to explicitly prohibit the use of its funds to induce firms to relocate from nearby jurisdictions (U.S. GAO 1996).

As a result, industrial location subsidies have been generally condemned in recent Bank reviews. Hon and Fallon's 2002 review of regional development incentives concluded that, in general, regional incentives merely "inject resources into places that are prone to failure." Shankar and Shah (2001) conclude, "regional policies have failed in almost all countries—federal and unitary alike."

CHAPTER 6

Custom-Tailored Approaches

The failure of firm-specific subsidies has prompted a move to a more comprehensive, tailor-made approach to regional development. This approach, as characterized by the World Bank,28 the EU, and the OECD (2005), is based on a diagnosis of a particular region's comparative advantages and the constraints on its development. The result is a strategy identifying key growth sectors and actions to be taken by various stakeholders, including national and local governments, private firms, and NGOs. OECD, for example, has completed an extensive series of territorial reviews aimed at analyzing factors that constrain the growth of specific regions within individual countries. These include the transportation network, the local business environment, and the constraints on local public service planning and management imposed by the structure of subnational government. They also identify prospective growth sectors. The OECD 2001 analysis of the Teruel region in Spain, for example, cites the region's unspoiled countryside and agricultural traditions to advocate an economic strategy based on the niche marketing of local products—ham, olives, and peaches—and farm-based tourism. OECD's 2002 analysis of the Moravska Trebova-Jevicsko region of the Czech Republic similarly, focuses on the niche marketing of agricultural products. EU regulations governing the allocation of Structural Funds in the 2007–2013 planning period now require the development of regional economic strategies.29

In principle, this customized, comprehensive approach to regional development makes a great deal of sense, given the wide range of factors that contribute to regional

---

28. See http://web.worldbank.org/WBSITE/EXTERNAL/TOPICS/EXTURBANDEVELOPMENT/EXTLED.
29. EU Council Regulation 2004/0163.

economic growth and the variety of circumstances in which regions find themselves. The situation of a collapsing one-industry town in southern Poland is a far cry from that of a persistently poor rural area in Eastern Anatolia. Regional development strategies would be expected to vary accordingly. The recent factor competitiveness study (Cambridge Econometrics 2002) prepared for DG-REGIO identified three types of regions, with corresponding development strategies: (i) production site regions, which can derive competitiveness from cheap inputs (low cost sites, absence of congestion, affordable housing and cheap labor); (ii) dynamic growth sector regions with industry-specific agglomeration economies, where the key advantages are labor skills and the availability of specialized services and specialized suppliers; and (iii) knowledge regions (large urban areas which can take advantage not only of industry-specific agglomeration economies, but cross sectoral agglomeration economies as well). To this list, one might add regions with no conceivable competitive advantage, where outmigration and social assistance are the only viable solutions to regional poverty.

A variety of analytical tools are available for the development of regional economic development strategies. Some of these have been developed in the field of regional science, regional planning, and economic geography. They range from traditional models—aimed at identifying the export base of a given region[30] and its impact on the wider regional economy—to general equilibrium models. They also include more eclectic approaches of the OECD type—aimed at inventorying natural advantages and infrastructure and institutional constraints.

Can Governments Pick Winners?

How far governments (or international financial institutions) should go in devising regional development strategies remains a subject of controversy. The arguments—pro and con—are similar to those surrounding industrial policy. The literature on industrial policy provides support for both sides of the argument. Rodrik (2004) summarizes the conventional arguments against industrial policies: "Governments cannot pick winners, developing countries lack the competent bureaucracies to render them effective, they are prone to political capture and corruption, there is little evidence that they work . . . and thanks to the WTO, they are illegal anyway." Pack and Saggi (2006) add that "the public sector is not omniscient, and in fact has even less information than the private sector about the nature of market failures." In his review of industrial policies, Pack and Saggi note that "that no one really knows whether any particular industry will eventually be profitable in a given situation. Such knowledge would require a knowledge of: (i) the industries that benefit from dynamic scale economies (i.e., learning by doing); (ii) the magnitude of the cost disadvantage at each stage of the learning process; (iii) the sectors that have long term competitiveness; (iv) the magnitude and scale of inter-industry spillovers; and (v) the extent to which early entrants generate benefits for future entrants." They state that "no study has attempted to assess whether governments have mastered these . . . areas" and conclude that "there is

---

30. For example, shift-share and location quotient analysis. These methods compare the sectoral composition of a region's economy with the sectoral composition of the national economy. Sectors that are over-represented in the region (with a location quotient over 1.0) are considered to be export sectors. It should be noted that usefulness of these tools for anything more than descriptive purposes is questionable.

not a single agreed counterfactual to evaluate the success of industrial policies targeted to individual industries. Researchers have examined the impact of trade protection, subsidies to R&D, general subsidies, and preferential lending rates on the evolution of productivity, capital accumulation and structure. Few of the empirical analyses find that sectoral targeting has been particularly effective."

There are cases where the public sector seems to have played an instrumental role in the development of particular sectors or regions. Chile's burgeoning fruit-exporting industry is a well known example. There, the Corporacion de Fomento (CORFO) played an important role in the early 1960s in surveying existing fruit orchards, analyzing potential demand in foreign markets, introducing and screening new varieties, establishing nurseries to propagate disease-free plants, constructing cold-storage facilities at strategic locations to promote post-harvest care, conducting sanitary inspections of exported fruit, and opening up favorable credit lines for working capital. Exports grew at an annual rate of 20 percent in the first 20 years of the reform. Areas planted to commercial orchards almost tripled and fruit production quadrupled (De Ferranti and others).

Korea's first comprehensive development plan (1972–81) not only picked winning sectors but winning regions where they should concentrate. Industrial decentralization was largely pursued for military reasons—Seoul is dangerously close to the North Korean border. The cities of Pohang, Changwon, Cyeoje, and Gumi were selected for heavy industry. Ulsan, on the southeastern coast, 70 km north of Busan, was assigned the leading role in chemicals and automobile manufacturing. Daegu became the textile center. This policy was codified in the Free Export Zone Establishment Law and Industrial Distribution Law of 1977, which called for the establishment of specialized economic zones near the coastal regions. At the outset, the government issued relocation orders. Yet, the relocation was largely accomplished through strategic partnerships with chaebols (industrial groups) offering tax incentives, training subsidies and tariff exemptions. This strategy worked—in the sense that the industries managed to thrive in their designated locations. The economic costs of this particular regional strategy are not known, however (Markusen 1995).

Ireland's initial development leap also involved a certain amount of sectoral targeting. Ireland was coming off half a century of economic stagnation when its economic boom began. The economy grew at an average rate of only two percent in the 1950s, far below the Western European average. In 1958, the Government began to replace its historically isolationist and protectionist policies with a policy of openness to trade and investment. In 1973, it joined the European Union, and in 1979, the European Monetary System, ending a fixed link to the British pound. Joining the EU had a dramatic impact on Ireland's economy. By reducing tariffs within the EU, it gave Irish products easier access to EU markets. It also increased Ireland's attractiveness as a base for foreign manufacturing investment, both for non-EU countries looking for a base to penetrate the EU market, and for EU firms looking for a cheap manufacturing base within the EU. Labor was another of Ireland's attractions. Relative to other EU countries, the labor force was young, relatively well educated, and cheap. Literacy among the young was virtually universal. Wage levels were low by northern European standards. (Although pay levels and conditions were generally agreed through collective bargaining between employees and employers, less than 20 percent of private sector employees were trade union members, and pay levels were largely market-determined.) The labor force was also English-speaking—an attraction not only to U.S. firms, but to other multinationals as English is the common language of multi-national corporations regardless of national origin. The Government topped these advantages with a program of industrial incentives. Prior to 1982 (and increasing EU restrictions) Ireland offered a full tax holiday on profits arising from new export sales by foreign manufacturing companies. The Government's efforts were particularly focused on electronics and pharmaceuticals, both "weightless" sectors[31] in which rapid growth was expected. In an effort to develop agglomeration economies, the Government also promoted "clusters" of related industries. Thus, computer assembly firms (Apple, Compaq, Dell, Gateway, and IBM) were followed by microprocessor manufacturers (Intel and NEC) and software companies (Microsoft, Lotus, and Oracle.) The rest is history.

However, these may be the exceptions. The fact that government intervention has been occasionally associated with success does not mean that all government interventions will have similar results. On this issue, Rodrik (2004) may have the last word. He advocates a relatively modest role for the public sector, a "flexible form of strategic collaboration between the public and private sectors, designed to elicit information about objectives and constraints on growth." Perhaps most importantly, he argues that the "trick is not to pick winners but to cut losses quickly when mistakes have been made."

A more modest approach would be to undertake the sort of investment climate assessments that the Bank now undertakes at the national level. These assessments benchmark factors that influence private investment decisions and identify improvements in the business-enabling environment for private enterprises. The Business Environment and Enterprise Performance Survey (BEEPS) survey, for example, generates comparative measurements in areas such as government relations (corruption and regulatory environment), labor, access to capital, legal and judicial issues, and infrastructure. World Bank investment climate assessments, now conducted at a national level, cover the range of issues that affect the development of specific regions as well. As shown in Box 7, the Moldova Investment Climate Assessment, for example, addresses the country's macroeconomic climate, foreign investors' perceptions of the investment climate, administrative and legal constraints, labor regulations and skills, access to finance, access to land, and a range of infrastructure services. Such studies can be expensive, however, and may not be feasible for all regions in all countries.

---

31. Sectors in which transport represents a small proportion of total production costs.

Box 7. Moldova Investment Climate Assessment

Table of Contents
1. From Recovery Growth to Sustainable Growth . . . .
   An Economy in Transition: The Collapse and Recovery of
      Moldova's Economy . . . .
   Evidence of an Unfinished Agenda . . . .
   Economic Growth and Poverty Alleviation Go Hand-in-Hand . . . .
2. Perceptions and Other Indicators of the Investment Climate
   Policy Uncertainty and Overburdening Regulations Among Top
      Concerns of Business . . . .
   The Cost of Doing Business–Highest Compliance Costs
      in the Region, Corruption. . . . .
   Policy Uncertainty: Selective Use of Regulations for Political
      and Economic Purposes. . . . .
3. Administrative and Legal Constraints . . . .
   Administrative Barriers–The Number One Problem
   Corruption–Not much Change . . . .
   Taxation–Reasonable Income Rates, High VAT and
      Unreasonable Administration . . . .
   Price Controls and Competition Policy. . . . .
   The Legal Environment. . . . .
   Customs and Trade Regulations—Another Constraint. . . . .
   Real Estate and Construction . . . .
4. Labor, Finance and Land. . . . .
   Labor. . . . .
   Finance . . . .
   Land . . . .
5. Infrastructure Services. . . . .
   Telecommunications. . . . .
   Transportation. . . . .
   Energy. . . . .
   Water. . . . .
6. Policy Recommendations . . . .
   Easing Burden of Regulations. . . . .
   Lightening Other Constraints. . . . .

CHAPTER 7

Planning and Allocating Funds for Regional Development

Regional development involves a wide range of sectors and political actors. As noted earlier, central governments typically set the policy framework for regional economic development: the national tax structure and trade regime, the terms and conditions of formal sector employment, and the social safety network, as well as the system of intergovernmental fiscal transfers. National sectoral ministries dominate the provision of national-scale infrastructure, such as highways, railroads, telecommunications, and energy. They also play a major financing role in education and health (in the latter case, through national insurance schemes). Municipal governments in the ECA region tend to be responsible for urban public utilities (i.e., water supply, sewerage, and district heating), along with solid waste management and the construction of city streets and rural feeder roads. In the majority of countries reviewed for this study, they are also responsible for the management of primary education and play a role in the management of primary health care facilities (although in both cases, funding is typically centrally provided.)

The problem, from a regional development standpoint, is to orchestrate the actions of these disparate actors in pursuit of a development strategy for a particular geographical area. National sectoral ministries, it is said, tend to operate in sectoral stovepipes without considering the wider economic development implications of their actions or possible synergies with other sectors. Municipal governments, in principle, are well positioned to take a cross-sectoral approach to economic development, but suffer from structural problems of their own. First, they are too small. As shown in Table 5, the average size of local governments in the ECA region tends to be less than 30,000. In the majority of ECA countries it is less than 10,000. As a result, locally-devised development strategies are likely to be too parochial. Individual municipal governments are unlikely to take region-wide benefits into consideration. In fact, they may find themselves competing against each other, rather than

Table 5. Average Population of Local Governments in Selected ECA Countries	
Country	Average Population
Czech Republic	1,659
Slovakia	1,855
Azerbaijan	3,057
Hungary	3,242
Latvia	4,400
Estonia	5,713
Romania	7,156
Albania	8,227
Slovenia	10,332
Russia	11,895
Poland	15,561
Turkey	21,589
Bulgaria	29,920
Serbia	46,570
Ukraine	51,248
Lithuania	66,300
Kazakhstan	71,783

Source: IMF and country reports. "Local government" excludes intermediate tiers (oblasts, provinces).

acting in concert. In addition, local governments—with the important exception of capital cities and major commercial centers (e.g., St. Petersburg, Almaty)—lack influence at the national level. They are not in a position to bend the behavior of national sectoral ministries to their will. While the municipal governments of major metropolitan areas might be well-positioned to prepare comprehensive development strategies, it is unlikely that each of the Czech Republic's 6,300 local governments (or Russia's 12,200, or Turkey's 3,225, etc.) would be capable of doing so.

Lessons from EU Structural Funds

The advent of EU funding for regional development has sparked a variety of experiments in regional planning in the western countries of the ECA region. Rules governing the 2000–2006 planning period affected the EU10 accession countries, which began accessing structural funds in 2004. Rules governing the 2007–2013 planning period will also affect Romania and Bulgaria, and influence prospective candidates, including Turkey.

According to the EU regulations governing the 2000–06[32] planning period, the process for programming structural funds should begin with the preparation of a development plan for each region. Separate plans are to be drawn up at the geographical level "deemed by the member state concerned to be most appropriate" but as a general rule, "covering a single region at the NUTS2 level."[33] These plans are to be based on "national and regional priorities" and include a precise description of the current situation in the region (disparities, lags, development potential) and a description of the "most appropriate strategy for achieving the development objectives for the region." Each plan is to

---

32. Council Regulation 1260/1999.

33. While some of the nomenclature has been changed for the 2007–2013 planning period, the rules governing the allocation of funds to individual regions remain essentially the same. Inter alia, the community support framework is now called the national strategic reference framework (NSRF). The former Objective 1 regions are now called 'convergence' regions but are still defined as regions with per capita GDPs below 75 percent of the EU average. The former Objective 2 regions are now 'competitiveness and employment' regions and consists of regions with per-capita GDPs *above* 75 percent of the EU average. Funds for the new trans-border cooperation objective (which accounts for a small share of the total) are available to either type of region, provided the project involves a region in another member state. The entire territories of the new member states are eligible for the funds allocated under the convergence objective, with the exception of the Prague region of the Czech Republic.

be appraised by the relevant member state, which then prepares a Community Support Framework showing the strategy and priorities for each of the structural funds, their specific objectives and indications as to how structural funds will be used in the particular region. The community support frameworks are then to be broken down into operational programs (OPs), consisting of multi-annual measures to be implemented through one or more of the structural funds. Although regulations require the OPs to "contain a description of the monitoring and evaluation system to be used" and the "procedures for the mobilization and circulation of financial flows" (for transparency purposes) they are not required to specify the allocation process or appraisal criteria that will be used to assign funds.

Poland

Member states reacted in different ways to this directive. The Polish case illustrates one response. For the 2004–2006 planning period, the process began with elaboration of a National Development Plan, laying out in extremely broad terms a diagnosis of the socio-economic situation, the extent of regional economic disparities, a strategy for national competitiveness, and an outline of operation programs and measures to be carried out within their scope. This was negotiated with the EU, and was the basis for Poland's sole community support framework as well as for the initial allocation of EU funds to the various operational programs.

Roughly one-third of Structural Funds were allocated to an Integrated Regional Operational Program (IROP). The documentation for this OP identified a wide array of activities eligible for EU financing. These were couched in terms of three broad priorities: development of infrastructure to enhance regional competitiveness, strengthening human resources, and local development. Although the IROP also provided a more detailed list of eligible measures and activities, this did little to limit the range of eligible projects (Ministry of Economy and Labor 2004).

Each of Poland's 16 NUTS2 regional governments—the voivodships—then prepared a regional strategy. Like the IROP, these did little to define priorities or narrow the range of possible projects. The Strategy for the Socio Economic Development of the Warminsko-Mazurskie Region, for example, specifies three broad priorities: (i) competitiveness; (ii) openness to ideas and innovations; and (iii) the development of modern networks, both physical (transport and telecommunications) and psychological (interpersonal contacts and cooperation). Each priority is broken down into actions; some of them referring to specific beneficiaries (firms, job seekers, external investors) and others to sectors (high quality foods, tourism, services for the elderly). Actions are further subdivided into sub-actions. The first action—increasing the competitiveness of firms—includes fifteen sub-actions, beginning with "support for the creation of technology transfer mechanisms" and ending with "dissemination of the concept of entrepreneurship and assistance in the creation of enterprises and support for development of newly created firms". In total, the strategy contains 248 such subactions eligible for financing.

The procedure used to allocate IROP funds to individual projects makes scant reference to the priorities defined in the planning process. Under the 2004–2006 program,

IROP funds were first allocated the voivodships. Each voivodship was allocated a fixed share of the total pool, largely on the basis of population.[34] Within each voivodship, funds were allocated on the basis of a seven step process:

- First, the voivodship issued a call for proposals to potential beneficiaries, including the two subordinate forms of local government (*gminas* and *powiats*), NGOs, and the agencies of the voivodship itself.
- Potential beneficiaries then submitted detailed project proposals, including detailed feasibility studies.
- The voivodship reviewed the proposals to ensure that all the forms, clearances, and financing arrangements were correctly documented.
- If so, the proposal was then submitted to a small expert panel, each member of which assigned a point score to each project, based on a standard table. The expert panel often consisted of two staff members from the voivodship, who lacked appropriate technical expertise and had little time to work.[35] The evaluation process typically occurred at the end of the normal workday and involved the panel meeting for four to five hours to undertake their joint assessment of two to three project proposals.
- Projects achieving at least a minimum number of points (generally 60) were referred to a steering committee, chaired by the chief executive of the voividship (the marshal) and including representatives of the subordinate local governments, the central government (including the Ministry of Economy and the Ministries of Infrastructure, Education, and Environment) and other interested parties. (The steering committee's role was purely advisory. It could not reject a project but could change its ranking.)
- After review by the steering committee, the proposal was then submitted to a board, consisting of the marshal and four senior managers from the voivodship. The Board had the final power to approve or reject individual projects.
- A project approved by the Board was then referred to the central government's representative at the voivodship level, who was responsible for signing the contract with the beneficiary, supervising implementation, and administering disbursements.

This process had several conspicuous weaknesses. Technical evaluations were too cursory. Political evaluations were too extensive. In addition, the procedure provided no mechanism to evaluate individual projects as part of a coherent regional strategy—even if one had existed. It also failed to integrate locally-initiated projects with the plans of

---

34. Eighty percent of the funds would be allocated on the basis of population with the remainder assigned to voivods where (i) per capita GDP is less than 80 percent of the national average or (ii) unemployment has been over 150 percent of the national average for the last three years).

35. The low level of compensation provided for the members of the expert panel effectively discouraged the participation of independent professionals. In one region, each expert was paid 100 PLN for evaluating two to three proposals. Assuming no preparation time outside of that meeting, this translates into about 4–5 Euro per hour of work.

national sectoral ministries. As a result, there appears to have been little that was "regional" in the allocation of regional EU funds.[36]

Ireland

Until recently, Ireland was a single region for purposes of EU structural funding. Its National Development Plans (NDPs) have doubled as its documentation for EU funding, including (in the 2000–2006 planning period) its community support framework. In principle, the 2000–2006 NDP was the result of a highly consultative process, including a joint analysis by the various stakeholders of the development needs of the country and sectoral investment priorities. But these partners appear to have participated mostly at the strategic level. There is no evidence, for example, of any formal mechanism for incorporating local governments' project proposals into the National Development Plan. (There did, however, appear to be informal points of access for stakeholders in Ireland's small scale, everybody-knows-everybody-else political culture.)[37]

The result was a National Development Plan that was clearly focused in both sectoral and geographical terms. The third National Development Plan, 2000–2006, was designed in an environment of full employment, but increasing congestion—evidence by traffic levels—and rising housing costs. On this basis, the National Development Plan recommended focusing capital investment on three main sectors: roads, housing and the environment. Geographical priorities were also clearly identified, with funding concentrated in Dublin and a limited number of other "gateway" cities.

Spain

While the Irish approach is considered highly successful (and, in fact, is singled out for praise in EU documentation) it is not clear that it would function as well in a larger, less homogenous context. Such is the case of Spain. At the national level, Spain's community support framework resembled those of countries to the east (e.g., Poland). In line with EU parlance, it defined eight "axes" of development. These were: (i) improving the

---

36. Although the evaluation process did award points for 'consistency with national strategic priorities', these priorities were so broadly defined that they provided little guidance or restraint. In the case reviewed for this study—a health project—the most important factor (up to 16 out of a potential 68 points) was 'consistency with the national health program and/or the voivodship strategy and/or the voivod health improvement program'. Points were also awarded for sustainability (up to eight points); use of performance indicators (four points); technical feasibility (four points); consistency with EU environmental, equal opportunity, and IT standards (five points); impact on health quality (eight points); impact on access to specialized health care (eight points); rationality, in epidemiological and demographic terms, of the location of the facilities (four points); responsiveness to emergencies and national disasters (eight points); and compatibility with other projects (four points).

37. This willingness to turn decision making power over to technocrats has been attributed to an underlying social consensus which was, in turn, a reaction to several decades of economic stagnation culminating in an economic crisis in the mid-1980's. The crisis was the catalyst for agreements on tough economic measures, hammered out through negotiations with trade unions, employers, farmers' organizations, NGOs, and politicians from across the political spectrum. These were codified in a series of social pacts. While the social pacts brought all the players to the table, they left the table with a consensus on broad strategic priorities but with the understanding that technical issues (including the programming of EU Structural Funds) will be turned over to the experts.

competitiveness and development of the production network; (ii) building a "knowledge society"; (iii) environment and natural resources; (iv) development of human resources and employability; (v) urban and local development; (vi) transport and energy networks; (vii) agriculture and rural development; and (viii) fishing and aquaculture. As required by EU guidelines, it included a table showing the breakdown of proposed spending, under each axis.

At the national level, the Ministry of Development (Infrastructure and Transport) played a major role in the identification of infrastructure projects to be proposed for EU funding. But in Spain's decentralized structure of government, the national government is not the only actor involved in the allocation of Structural Funds. The seventeen regional governments also played a major role.

The Andalucia regional government, for example, prepared its own regional economic plan (Junta de Andalucia 2002). Like the national plan, this identified generic "axes" for development: (i) improving the competitiveness and development of the production network; (ii) knowledge and telecommunication; (iii) environment and natural resources; (iv) development of human resources and employability; (v) urban and local development; (vi) transport and energy networks; (vii) agriculture and rural development; (viii) fishing and aquaculture; (ix) tourism; and (x) construction of collective infrastructure (meaning public toilets and social service centers). The regional plan was accompanied by an integrated operating program, which (like the national plan) included a breakdown of proposed spending for each axis.

As in Poland, these plans appear to have had relatively little impact on the selection of individual projects. Instead, the Andalucian Ministry (Consejeria) of Economy, as well as the regional Ministry of Works, played the dominant role in project identification and selection. Officially, the first step in the process was to meet with social agents: trade unions, entrepreneurs, consumer groups, provincial representatives of regional ministries, and the federation of municipalities. As in Ireland, this appears to have been a general consensus building exercise, with little input on particular projects. The instruments that directly affect the allocation of funding to specific projects were the Ministry of Works' medium term investment plan and the annual budget of the regional government. Mayors seeking project funding had to submit their proposals to the Ministry's delegate at the provincial level, who could choose to pass it to the minister in Seville—who then could choose whether to include it in the rolling medium term investment plan and in the ministry's annual budget submission to the regional government.

The two-tier structure of development planning in Spain has required considerable coordination between Madrid and the regional governments. They appear to have arrived at a workable modus operandi. Once Spain's overall level of structural funds was negotiated with Brussels, the amount was divided among the 17 regions, largely on the basis of population and level of economic development.[38] Each region's share was then divided between projects to be executed by central government and those to be executed by regional governments. These shares largely reflected historical precedent and ranged from 40:60 to 60:40. Within its spending envelope, each region was then relatively free to allocate funds according to its own priorities.

---

38. Several of the regions in the northeast are no longer eligible for EU funds under Objective 1.

Box 8. Regional Development Agencies in Turkey

In anticipation of EU accession, Turkey has divided its national territory into 26 NUTS2 regions. With three exceptions (Istanbul, Izmir, and Ankara) each region includes at least two—and as many as six—of Turkey's traditional units of intermediate government—the provinces. Under the recently enacted regional development law, each region is to have a regional development agency (RDA) which will be responsible for drawing up and overseeing the implementation of a regional development plan. Although the process is at an early stage (only two RDAs had been established as of December 2006) institutional problems are already foreseeable. Because most of NUTS2 regions include several provinces, the RDAs are likely to run afoul of rivalries among the provinces that comprise them. At the same time, they will have difficulty coordinating the activities of national sectoral ministries in Turkey's highly centralized public sector. In principle, this function is performed by the State Planning Organization (SPO). But the SPO itself is largely organized along sectoral lines. Although the SPO has a regional development department, its activities are largely confined to the management of EU funds and other special projects.

Regional development agencies have been known to operate successfully in a more limited role—that of regional investment promotion. In that regard, they prepare informational brochures on their region and present them at trade fairs; they cold-call firms that appear to be likely targets; they roll out the welcome wagon for investors who express an interest in investing in their region, meeting them at the airport, showing them potential sites that meet their needs—and they assist them, once they move in with getting licenses and finding qualified staff. These seem to be low-cost and clearly useful actions.

In theory, a similar approach could be tried in the ECA countries. With four exceptions (Estonia, Lithuania, Serbia, and Slovenia[39]) every country in the ECA region has at least one intermediate tier of government. Some have several. As noted earlier, Poland has 16 provinces (voivodships). These are in turn divided into 373 counties (*powiats*), which are in turn divided into 2,900 communes and city governments. But intermediate tiers of government in ECA countries are weak. Some are merely councils of mayors. Some, until recently, existed only to coordinate the activities of national sectoral ministries. Most have extremely limited functions. The responsibilities of Latvia's 26 rayons, for example, are largely confined to managing public transport services and funding for roads. Poland's powiats are responsible for secondary education and (together with the voivodships) certain aspects of social assistance. Even in the Russian Federation, the spending of the 89 units of federation is exceeded by that of the rayons and municipalities. Under these circumstances, it is not clear that intermediate tiers of government would be in a position to exercise the role performed by the regional governments in Spain. In fact, there is some risk that efforts to create intermediate tiers of government in anticipation of EU funding may create more problems than they solve. This may be in case in Turkey, as described in Box 8.

The OECD's recent report (2005) on building competitive regions proposes the use of intergovernmental contracts as a means of orchestrating the activities of various tiers of government. It cites the model of French state-region plan contracts (CPER). According to the OECD, these are hammered out through lengthy negotiations between two sets of parties: (i) the elected local and regional authorities and other "development actors in the

---

39. Serbia has one provincial government, serving the northern part of the country—Voivodina. In the rest of the country, municipalities constitute the only level of subnational government.

region" and (ii) a regional "prefect" who is designated by the State. All such regional programs are coordinated by the State Delegation for Territorial Management and Regional Action. Each national sectoral ministry forms a steering committee to coordinate its contribution to the program. This mechanism has a well-established track record in France. Successive five year contracts have been in effect in all French regions since 1984. The OECD notes, however, that such contracts involve high costs in terms of negotiation and execution. At the time the OECD report was written, it was expected that the current contracts (covering the period 2000–06) would have to be extended into 2007 due to administrative delays. It is also not clear that this approach, adapted to the French system of intergovernmental relations (in which, *inter alia*, politicians are permitted to hold office simultaneously at the local, regional, and central level), would function as well in the more rigid, and often confrontational, systems of intergovernmental relations to the East.

Full analysis of the organizational issues posed by regional development is beyond the scope of this report. But the available evidence supports some tentative conclusions. First, as a device for coordinating the actions of multiple tiers of government in pursuit of a regional development strategy, the Spanish approach has much to recommend it. But the success of the Spanish approach owes much to its political and institutional context. It is unlikely to work where intermediate levels of governments do not constitute a large share of total public spending and are not in a position to drive a hard bargain with national sectoral ministries and the national political leadership. Creating artificial regional organizations to define regional development strategies and allocate funds for regional development does not appear to be an attractive alternative. Under these circumstances, the best alternative may be to leave each tier of government to do its own planning in its areas of functional responsibility—and to improve the procedures for individual project selection.

Improving Individual Project Evaluation

With or without a strong regional coordinating mechanism, there is clearly a case for improving the quality of individual project evaluation—whether this is undertaken by individual municipal governments, national sectoral ministries, or an intermediate tier. There is a fairly extensive literature on project evaluation, including the Bank's own contributions. Much of this is justly criticized for advocating approaches that are unrealistically complicated. In theory, it might be desirable for every project to emerge from a comprehensive and participatory analysis of regional development needs, carefully integrated with the plans of national ministries and other stakeholders, and then appraised according to rigorous economic, social, and environmental criteria. Yet, this is likely to be administratively impractical, particularly where it involves hundreds of individual projects.

Three more modest recommendations emerge from the literature. First, governments should establish clear, consistent appraisal criteria up front—appraisal methodologies and thresholds for acceptability that have to be met before a project can be considered for funding. Techniques should be commensurate with the size of the project and its complexity. One source (Fitzpatrick Associates 1999) notes that even the most sophisticated cost-benefit analysis is more useful in posing difficult questions than providing definitive rankings. As discussed in Box 9, the Chilean government has developed project evaluation to a high art—although at some cost in terms of administrative overhead.

Box 9. Project Evaluation in Chile

In Chile, every Government-funded investment expenditure—including those of subnational governments and central government ministries—must be evaluated by the Ministry of Planning (MIDEPLAN) before it can be submitted for funding consideration in the annual budget process. MIDEPLAN's appraisal criteria are exhaustively defined in a project appraisal manual, termed SEBI. This specifies, for each subsector, a precise methodology for calculating costs and benefits. The evaluation methodology for primary health centers, for example runs to 271 pages. The evaluation methodology for streets (as opposed to intercity roads or rural roads) runs to a more modest 48 pages. Basic cost factors—including social prices for labor, capital costs and foreign exchange—are issued by MIDEPLAN and updated at least once a year. MIDEPLAN manages to process an average of 20,000 project proposals through this system annually. Of this total, 8,000 proposals are immediately excluded due to incomplete documentation. Of the remaining 12,000, roughly 40 percent are typically approved—subject to financing. Three thousand make it into the budget. While this system is reportedly highly successful at excluding economically unjustifiable projects from budget consideration, it involves considerable administrative costs. One hundred sixty staff are reportedly employed in the project evaluation function.

Second, the staff responsible for evaluation must be competent and sufficiently insulated from political pressure. The terms and conditions of staff must be sufficient to attract and retain technically competent staff. To ensure that staff are independent as well as technically competent, their appointment must be made by a party not likely to be beholden to the same political pressures as the entities proposing the projects. Some countries rely extensively on consultants to perform this role. Others rely on staff of national sectoral ministries to evaluate projects proposed by local governments.

Third, the timing and extent of non-technical influences on project selection must be well defined. The selection of capital investment projects involves judgment. It involves choices among priorities that cannot be made solely on the basis of rate-of-return calculations. Potential beneficiaries and their political representatives therefore have an important role to play in the project selection process. But this role should be constrained. In all of the countries reviewed for this part of the study, the ultimate choice of projects to be funded in the national annual budget rests either with a council of ministers, with parliament, or with their equivalents at the local or regional levels. In some cases, their selections are unconstrained. Parliamentarians can choose among hundreds or thousands of projects which have received only cursory technical reviews. They can add new projects of their own and change the rating on projects proposed by sectoral ministries. In other countries, the choice of projects to be funded in the annual budget is limited to those which have met minimum thresholds—in economic, financial, and engineering terms. The latter approach has much to recommend it.

CHAPTER 8

Conclusions

Regional development means different things to different people. In evaluating a government's regional development efforts, it is important to understand the government's motivations. Is it trying to reduce persistent concentrations of poverty in remote regions? Or is it trying to defuse secessionist demands or slow the growth of major cities? Is it seeking development strategies that will unlock the economic potential of a particular region for benefit of the nation as a whole? Or a more parochial effort that may merely shift jobs from one region to another? Under some conditions, efforts to address poverty through regional development are justifiable. Efforts to defuse secessionist demands or slow migration are more difficult to assess. Where these are among the government's objectives, it is important to minimize collateral economic damage.

Efforts to address regional concentrations of poverty should begin by considering whether the problem would be best resolved through regional economic development or through more direct forms of income support and social spending. If poverty is the result of demography—age profiles that render residents too young or too old to participate in the labor force—efforts to bring higher wage employment to poor regions will have little benefit for the resident population. Efforts to reduce poverty should instead focus on providing income support to households with large numbers of unemployable dependents and on improving educational opportunities for school-age children—if only to prepare them to migrate to places with better job prospects.

If the problem is not solely demographic—if the region has a working age population that merely lacks well-paying employment opportunities—consideration should be given to removing impediments to factor mobility. This might include the abolition of nationally uniform minimum wages and industry-wide collective bargaining practices, so that firms have an incentive to invest in locations with cheap but productive labor. It might include cuts in

unemployment benefits and other forms of social protection to encourage working-age people in lagging regions to migrate. It might also include housing policy reforms (including the
abolition of rent control) to increase the supply of housing in potential destination regions.
This does not guarantee that economically declining regions will begin to grow. But it does
hold out the promise that poor people in declining regions will have higher-paying employment opportunities—even if they have to migrate elsewhere to get them.

There are nevertheless valid arguments for extending special treatment to regions with
high concentrations of poverty. Factor mobility alone is unlikely to eliminate pockets of
poverty within a relevant time frame. Cultural barriers impede migration. Cultural values may
make migration a socially unacceptable solution. By the same token, the underdeveloped
capital markets of some ECA countries are not likely to seek out high-return investments on
their own initiative. Individual investors cannot be expected to address constraints on infrastructure and human capital. But efforts at intervention have to be carefully assessed in terms
of their effectiveness.

The literature on economic geography argues fairly persuasively that, in market
economies, economic activity locates where it does for very good reasons. Scholars may argue
over the nature of initial comparative advantages and the relative importance of plant level,
industry level, and city-level agglomeration economies. But few dispute the notion that economic imperatives cause economic activity to concentrate in some regions and not in others. It follows that government efforts to alter the location of economic activity are likely to
be ineffective or extremely expensive—in terms of the government's budget and in terms of
the efficiency of the economy as a whole.

The literature also suggests that some of the traditional blunt instruments used to stimulate regional economic growth are not particularly effective. New highways can stimulate
regional exports, but they can also stimulate imports into the region—devastating local
industries. Firm-specific investment incentives also have a mixed track record. The evidence suggests that such incentives can affect investors' location decisions if the incentives
are large enough. But they do not guarantee that the investments will have broader multiplier effects on the regional economy. Or that the investors will remain once the incentives
run out.

Comprehensive, custom tailored approaches appear to be a promising alternative. In
principle, these are based on detailed diagnoses of the specific impediments to growth in a
particular region. They define key growth sectors and actions to be taken to stimulate those
sectors by central and local governments, business associations, community groups, and
other actors. But efforts by governments (or international organizations, consulting firms,
or NGOs) to pick "growth sectors" have a mixed track record. It is also not clear that countries are organized to implement comprehensive regional strategies. Most individual municipalities are too small. Few ECA countries have strong regional governments. Efforts to create
regional planning agencies run the risk of generating political orphans—ignored by both
national sectoral ministries and the local governments whose efforts they are supposed to
coordinate.

Governments should be therefore modest in using regional development as a tool of
poverty alleviation Focusing on geographically-defined units of analysis can be a useful device
for identifying constraints on poverty reduction that affect particular locations. Under some
circumstances, it can be a useful means of targeting poverty whose particular cause is location specific. But policies aimed at stimulating growth in poor regions have to be comple-

mented by more direct anti-poverty measures, including the improved targeting of transfers to low income households and investments in education and local services. Barriers to the out-migration of labor must be reduced. And barriers to the in-migration of capital—including national level reforms in the financial sector, business regulation, and in the organizations responsible for the timely provision of infrastructure and social services—must also be considered.

Poverty reduction is not, of course, the sole objective of regional policy. Environmental and social considerations are also important. Territorial integrity is another factor. Further work on these aspects of regional development deserves serious consideration.

Bibliography

Andrienkol, Yuri, and Sergei Guriev. 2004. "Determinants of interregional mobility in Russia." *The Economics of Transition* 12(1):1–192.

Armstrong, Harvey, and Jim Taylor. 2000. *Regional Economics and Policy Third Edition.* Oxford: Blackwell Publishing.

Aschauer, David Alan. 1989. "Is Public Expenditure Productive?" *Journal of Monetary Economics* 2(March):177–200.

Basile, Roberto, Sergio de Nardis, and Alessandro Girardi. 2004. *Regional Inequalities and Cohesion Policies in the European Union.* ISAE Instituto di Studi e Analisi Economica, Rome.

Beaudry, C., and others. 2000. "Clusters, Innovation and Growth: a Comparative Study of European Countries." Working Paper. Manchester Business School.

Boldrin, Michele, and Fabio Canova. 2003. "Regional Policies and EU Enlargement." Center for Economic Policy Research. Discussion Paper No. 3744.

Bradley, John. 2005. "Has EU Regional Policy Been Effective? The Debate on Structural Funds." Economic and Social Research Institute, Dublin.

Burgess, Robin, and Anthony Venables. 2004. "Toward a Microeconomics of Growth." In Francois Bourguignon and Boris Pleskovic, eds. *Accelerating Development: Annual World Bank Conference on Development Economics 2004.* Washington, D.C.: The World Bank.

Button, Kenneth. 2002. "The Role of Infrastructure in Promoting Growth and Development in Lagging Regions." Paper presented at the World Bank Workshop on "Promoting Growth and Development in Lagging Regions." Unpublished draft.

Cambridge Econometrics, ECORYS-NEI, and Ronald Martin. 2002. "A Study on the Factors of Regional Competitiveness: Draft Final Report for the European Commission Directorate-General Regional Policy." Cambridge UK.

Canning, David, and Pedroni, Peter. July 1999. *Infrastructure and Long Run Economic Growth.* Cornell University Center for Analytic Economics. Ithaca, NY: Cornell University.

Cappelen, Aadne, and others. 2003. "The Impact of EU Regional Support on Growth and Convergence in the European Union." *Journal of Common Market Studies* 41(4).

CEPR (Center for Economic Policy Research). n.d. "Regional Cohesion Evidence and Theories of Regional Growth and Convergence." CEPR Discussion Paper 1075. London, UK.

Combes, P., and M. Lafourcade. n.d. "Transportation Costs Decline and Regional Inequalities: Evidence from France 1978–1993." CEPR Discussion Paper 2894 London, UK.

Cortright, Joseph, 2006. *Making Sense of Clusters: Regional Competitiveness and Economic Development.* Brookings Institution, Washington, D.C.

De Ferranti, David, Guillermo Perry, Daniel Lederman, and William F. Maloney. 2002. *From Natural Resources to the Knowledge Economy.* Washington, D.C.: The World Bank.

De la Fuente. 2003. "Does Cohesion Policy Work?" In Bernard Funck and Lodovico Pizzati, eds., *European Integration, Regional Policy, and Growth.* Washington, D.C.: The World Bank.

ECOTEC Research and Consulting. No date. "Ex-Post Evaluation of Objective 1: A Final Report to the Directorate General for Regional Policy." European Commission, Brussels, Belgium.

European Commission Regional Policy Directorate. 2006. "Community Strategic Guidelines on Cohesion 2007–2013." http://ec.europa.eu/regional_policy/intro/working1_en.htm.

———. 1999. EU Council Regulation 1260/1999. http://ec.europa.eu/regional_policy/intro/working1_en.htm.

———. 2004. EU Council Regulation 2004/0163. http://ec.europa.eu/regional_policy/intro/working1_en.htm.

Faini, R. 1983. "Cumulative Processes of Deindustrialization in an Open Region: The Case of Southern Italy 1951–1973." *Journal of Development Economics* 12(3).

Feldmann, Horst. 2004. "How Flexible are Labor Markets in the EU Accession Countries Poland, Hungary and the Czech Republic?" *Comparative Economic Studies* 46(2).

Fitzpatrick Associates. 1999. *Review of Project Selection Procedures and Appraisal Techniques in the (Irish) Community Support Framework.* Dublin.

Fujita, Masahisa, Paul Krugman, and Anthony J. Venables. 1999. *The Spatial Economy: Cities, Regions and International Trade.* Cambridge, Mass.: MIT Press.

Fujita, Masahisa, and Jacques-Francois Thiesse. 2002. *The Economics of Agglomeration—Cities, Industrial Location, and Regional Growth.* Cambridge University Press.

Funck, Bernard, Lodovico Pizzati, and Martin Burncko. 2003. "Overview." In Bernard Funck and Lodovico Pizzati, eds., *European Integration, Regional Policy, and Growth.* Washington, D.C.: The World Bank.

Garnier, Carole. 2005. "Can Policy Instruments be Used to Encourage Subnational Development?" Background paper prepared for World Bank Workshop on Promoting Growth Development in Lagging Regions, June 3.

Glaeser, Edward L. 2003. "The New Economics of Urban and Regional Growth." In Gordon Clarke, Meric S. Gertler, and Maryann P. Feldman, *The Oxford Handbook of Economic Geography.* Oxford: Oxford University Press.

Hanson, Gordon. 2000. "Geographic Concentration." In Gordon Clarke and others, *The Oxford Handbook of Economic Geography.* Oxford: Oxford University Press.

Harris, J., and M. Todaro. 1970. "Migration, Unemployment & Development: A Two-Sector Analysis." *American Economic Review* 60(1):126–42.

Harrison, B., and others. 1996. "Innovative Firm Behavior and Local Milieu: Exploring the Intersection of Agglomeration, Firms Effects, and Technological Change." *Economic Geography* 72.

Henderson, V. 1997. "Externalities and Industrial Development." *Journal of Urban Economics* 42:449–79.

———. 2003. "Marshall's Scale Economies." *Journal of Urban Economics* 53(1):1–28.

Herve, Yves. 2000. "Intergovernmental Transfers as a Macroeconomic Success Story of European Integration: Myth or Reality?" University of Edinburgh, Europa Institute.

Hon, V., and Peter Fallon. 2003. "Regional Development Policies: Theory and a Review of the Evidence." Unpublished background paper prepared for the World Bank's "Maranhao (Brazil) State Economic Memorandum."

Huber, Peter. 2006. "Regional Labor Market Developments in Transition." World Bank Policy Research Working Paper No. 3896. The World Bank, Washington, D.C.

Johnson, Simon, John McMillan, and Christopher Woodruff. 2002. "Property Rights and Finance." John Olin Program in Law and Economics Working Paper 231. University of Chicago Law School, Chicago.

Junta de Andalucia. 2002. *Plan Economico Andalucia Siglo XXI 2002–2005*. Sevilla: Consejeria de Economia y Hacienda.

Krugman, Paul. 2000. "Where in the World is the New Economic Geography?" In Gordon Clarke and others, *The Oxford Handbook of Economic Geography*. Oxford: Oxford University Press.

Lucas, Robert. 1988. "On the Mechanics of Economic Development." *Journal of Monetary Economics* 22(1).

———. 2002. "Migration and Lagging Regions." Unpublished paper prepared for the World Bank.

Marcusen, Ann. 1995. "Interaction between Regional and Industrial Policies: Evidence from Four Countries." *Proceedings of the Annual World Bank Conference on Development Economics*. Washington, D.C.: The World Bank.

Martin, Philippe. 1998. "Can Regional Policies Affect Growth and Geography in Europe?" *The World Economy* 21(6):757–74.

———. 2003. "Public Policies and Economic Geography" In Bernard Funck and Lodovico Pizzati, eds., *European Integration, Regional Policy, and Growth*. Washington, D.C.: The World Bank.

Martin, R., and Peter Sunley. 2003. "Deconstructing Clusters: Chaotic Concept or Policy Panacea?" *Journal of Economic Geography* 3.

Ministry of Economy and Labor (Poland). 2004. *Poland Integrated Regional Operational Program 2004–2006*.

Myrdal, Gunnar. 1957. *Economic Theory and Underdeveloped Regions*. London: Duckworth.

OECD. 2001. "Territorial Reviews: Teruel, Spain." Paris.

———. 2002. "Territorial Reviews: Moravska Trebova-Jevicsko, Czech Republic." Paris.

———. 2005. "Building Competitive Regions: Strategies and Governance." Paris.

Pack, Howard, and Kamal Saggi. 2006. "Is There a Case for Industrial Policy? A Critical Survey." *The World Bank Research Observer* 21(2).

Porter, Michael. 2000. "Locations, Clusters and Company Strategy." In Gordon Clarke and others, *The Oxford Handbook of Economic Geography*. Oxford: Oxford University Press.

Rice, P. G., A. J. Venables, and E. Pattachine. 2006. "Spatial Determinants of Productivity, Analysis for the UK Regions." *Regional Science and Urban Economics* 36:727–52.

Rodrik, Dani. 2004. *Industrial Policy for the Twenty-First Century*. Cambridge, Mass.: John F. Kennedy School of Government.

Rosenthal, S. S., and W. C. Strange. 2004. "Evidence on the Nature and Sources of Agglomeration Economies." In V. Henderson and J. Thiesse, *Handbook of Urban and Regional Economics*. Amsterdam: Elsevier.

Sala-i-Martin, Xavier X. 1996. "Regional Cohesion: Evidence and Theories of Regional Growth and Convergence." *European Economic Review* 40:1325–52.

Sapir, Andre, and others. 2003. *An Agenda for a Growing Europe: Making the EU Economic System Deliver*. www.euractiv.com/ndbtext/innovation/sapirreport.pdf.

Shankar, Raja, and Anwar Shah. 2001. "Bridging the Economic Divide within Nations: A Scorecard on the Performance of Regional Development Policies in Reducing Regional Income Disparities." World Bank Policy and Research Working Paper No. 2717. The World Bank, Washington, D.C.

Stierle, Michael. 2004. "Conditions for a Contribution by the Structural Funds to Real Convergence of the Recently Acceded Member States." European Regional Science Association Conference Paper.

U.S. GAO (General Accounting Office). 1996. "Limited Information Exists on the Impact of Assistance Provided by Three Agencies." www.gao.gov/archive/1996/rc96103.pdf.

Vandycke, Nancy. 2001. *Access to Education for the Poor in Europe and Central Asia*. World Bank Technical Paper No. 511. Washington, D.C.: The World Bank.

Venables, A. J., 2006. "Shifts in Economic Geography and Their Causes." Paper prepared for 2006 Jackson Hole Symposium. www.kc.frb.org/PUBLICAT/SYMPOS/2006/pdf/venables.paper.0821.pdf

Williamson, J. 2000. "What Should the World Bank Think About the Washington Consensus?" *The World Bank Research Observer* 15(2).

World Bank. 1994. *World Development Report: Infrastructure for Development*. Washington, D.C.

———. 2004a. *Growth, Employment, and Living Standards in Poland*. Washington, D.C.

———. 2004b. "Local Economic Development: A Primer—Developing and Implementing Local Economic Development Strategies and Action Plan." WBSITE/EXTERNAL/TOPICS/EXTURBANDEVELOPMENT/EXTLED/0,,contentMDK:20276743~menuPK:341145~pagePK:148956~piPK:216618~theSitePK:341139,00.htmlE

———. 2004c. *Poland: Directions in Regional Policy*. Washington, D.C.

———. 2005a. *Enhancing Job Opportunities: Eastern Europe and the Former Soviet Union*. Washington, D.C.

———. 2005b. *Growth, Poverty and Inequality: Eastern Europe and the Former Soviet Union*. Washington, D.C.

———. 2006. *Internal Migration and Commuting in the New Member States of the EU*. Washington, D.C.

———. 2007a. Global Development Finance Database. Washington, D.C.

———. 2007b. http://web.worldbank.org/WBSITE/EXTERNAL/TOPICS/EXTURBAN DEVELOPMENT/EXTLED

Eco-Audit

Environmental Benefits Statement

The World Bank is committed to preserving Endangered Forests and natural resources. We print World Bank Working Papers and Country Studies on 100 percent postconsumer recycled paper, processed chlorine free. The World Bank has formally agreed to follow the recommended standards for paper usage set by Green Press Initiative—a nonprofit program supporting publishers in using fiber that is not sourced from Endangered Forests. For more information, visit www.greenpressinitiative.org.

In 2006, the printing of these books on recycled paper saved the following:

Trees*	Solid Waste	Water	Net Greenhouse Gases	Total Energy
203	9,544	73,944	17,498	141 mil.
'40" in height and 6-8" in diameter	Pounds	Gallons	Pounds CO_2 Equivalent	BTUs